VICE PRESIDENT
KAMALA HARRIS

VICE PRESIDENT
KAMALA HARRIS

HER PATH TO THE WHITE HOUSE

Introduction & Text by MALAIKA ADERO

Photo Editor CHRISTOPHER MEASOM

STERLING
New York

STERLING
New York

An Imprint of Sterling Publishing Co., Inc.

ISBN: 978-1-4549-4378-5
ISBN: 978-1-4549-4379-2 (e-book)

Distributed in Canada by Sterling Publishing Co., Inc.
c/o Canadian Manda Group, 664 Annette Street
Toronto, Ontario M6S 2C8, Canada
Distributed in the United Kingdom by GMC Distribution Services
Castle Place, 166 High Street, Lewes, East Sussex BN7 1XU, England
Distributed in Australia by NewSouth Books
University of New South Wales, Sydney, NSW 2052, Australia

For information about custom editions, special sales, and premium and
corporate purchases, please contact Sterling Special Sales at 800-805-5489
or specialsales@sterlingpublishing.com.

Manufactured in China

2 4 6 8 10 9 7 5 3 1

sterlingpublishing.com

Interior design by NightandDayDesign.biz

Cover design by Elizabeth Mihaltse Lindy

Picture Credits — see page 186

Previous pages: Democratic vice presidential candidate Senator Kamala
Harris at a campaign event in Las Vegas, October 27, 2020.

Contents

I'm Speaking

Women in the American sea of social change have been like water, necessary and appreciated within limits, but often disrespected and taken for granted. They gather, move, and grow over time and distance, with steps forward and steps back, rarely equated with power until they crash into the status quo so dramatically that the landscape they wash over bears little resemblance to what was there before.

The election of a woman, Kamala Devi Harris, for the first time ever to the second highest office in the land, signals that a new height has been reached in American politics, another glass ceiling shattered.

Since 1872, when Victoria Claflin Woodhull ran for president as the candidate for the Equal Rights Party, and as recently as 2016, when Hillary Rodham Clinton was the first woman running for president on a major party ticket, women have pursued but never won a seat in our executive branch of government. Internationally, women have been leading their nations for decades: Indira Gandhi in India, Golda Meir in Israel, Margaret Thatcher in England, Benazir Bhutto in Pakistan, Ellen Johnson Sirleaf in Liberia, and Angela Merkel in Germany. The United States has finally caught the wave, inaugurating Kamala Harris as vice president in 2021.

Opposite: Senator Kamala Harris in New York, April 5, 2019.

A vice presidential nominee representing a major American party is of course dependent on being chosen by the head of a party's ticket. Joe Biden's selection of a woman as his running mate was not precedent setting, as Geraldine Ferraro was selected by Walter Mondale in 1984; it was the victory of the Biden-Harris ticket in the 2020 election that set the new precedent. As Vice President Kamala Harris said in her victory speech, "While I may be the first woman in this office, I will not be the last."

The job of vice president of the United States has not always been viewed as an enviable one. The men who served before had varied opinions. The first vice president, John Adams, complained that it is "the most insignificant Office that ever the Invention of Man contrived, or his Imagination conceived." Woodrow Wilson's vice president, Thomas Marshall, once retired said, "I don't want to work . . . [but] I would not mind being Vice President again."

The role has evolved, like every other aspect of our democracy, and our forty-sixth president is well aware of it, being in the respected tradition of elected officials who read and pay attention to history. Biden is well aware that every American vice president has been white and male, including him, so how he integrates Harris into his administration will be closely watched. When Barack Obama selected him as his vice president, Biden made clear that he wanted an active role that would make use of his already long experience as a lawmaker, to be "the last voice in the room." So, when he offered the position on the ticket to Kamala Harris, he told her he wanted the same for her, that she would be the first and the last in the room, and have authority to "challenge [his] assumptions if she disagrees," and to "ask the hard questions." The job would not just be a ceremonial one.

The outdoor inauguration in front of the US Capitol on Wednesday, January 20, 2021, was like no other on a multitude of levels. Start with the fact that it occurred after a horrific riot in the same location just fourteen days earlier and while Americans were still in the throes of dealing with the worst pandemic in over one hundred years. Despite these conditions, this was the setting for the transfer of power to the new administration when Joseph Robinette Biden Jr. would become our forty-sixth president and Kamala Devi Harris would be sworn into

Kamala Harris marching with her family in the Inauguration Day parade in Washington, DC, January 20, 2021. From left: Her niece Meena's partner, Nikolas Ajagu, carrying their daughter Leela in his arms; Kamala Harris's brother-in-law, Tony West; Kamala Harris, holding her grandniece Amara's hand; Harris's niece, Meena; the vice president's husband, Second Gentleman Doug Emhoff; and Doug Emhoff's daughter, Ella Emhoff.

her office by the first Latina Supreme Court Justice, Sonia Sotomayor. When Harris took the oath, she made history in a multitude of ways: Not only was the first woman, first African American, and first Asian American elected to the office of vice president, but she and her husband, Second Gentleman Douglas Emhoff, who is Jewish, along with their blended family, would become the first interracial and interfaith Second Family. Perhaps it is a most fitting outcome after a year like 2020—characterized by a pandemic, uprisings, and a record-breaking rise in hate crimes by white nationalists.

Harris laid her hands on two Bibles for her swearing-in on Inauguration Day. One belonged to Regina Shelton, a family friend who was a surrogate mother to her when she was growing up in the Bay Area. The other belonged to her hero and inspiration, the late Justice Thurgood Marshall.

She said: "I, Kamala Devi Harris, do solemnly swear that I will support and defend the Constitution of the United States against all enemies, foreign and domestic; that I will bear true faith and allegiance to the same; that I take this obligation freely, without any mental reservation or purpose of evasion; that I will well and faithfully discharge the duties of the office upon which I am about to enter: So help me God."

Her first name, Kamala, is the Hindu word for *lotus*, a flower whose long, slender petals project from its stamen like a crown. It rests on a pad of leaves that float on water, looking ever so delicate but belying how strongly rooted it is in the mud. "Pluck it out," said an Indian-born English professor I had many years ago, "and the flower emerges from the mud." Kamla's middle name, Devi, translates to *mother*, *goddess*, *female energy*. Harris of course brings those qualities to her position as the highest-ranking female official in US history. She certainly looked ready for the role on Inauguration Day with her family at her side.

The presenters at this most emblematic American political ritual included singers Lady Gaga, wearing a hand-size gold peace dove brooch; Jennifer Lopez, in head-to-toe Chanel; and Garth Brooks, in jeans and a black cowboy hat. Amanda Gorman, a petite, heretofore little-known poet, our first National Youth Poet Laureate, upstaged everyone. Bringing tears to many guests' eyes was the appearance in the procession of US Capitol Police officer Eugene Goodman, who would later receive a Congressional Gold Medal for his heroic action protecting the Congress during the deadly January 6 siege when our democracy was threatened, lives were lost, and our elected leaders on both sides of the aisle were turned into victims.

The attendees looked like the multicultural society that the United States of America is, even though they were fewer in number than usual at such a historic event. That was not because Biden and Harris were unpopular; they were elected by more than 81 million voters, the most votes ever recieved by a presidential nominee. Whereas 1.8 million people attended Obama's first inauguration in 2009, security and safety measures limited attendance at the 2021 inauguration to one thousand select guests, who all wore the masks that have become a universal shield and political symbol.

The transfer of power from one American presidential administration and one political party to another was celebrated without incident, proving that our 245-year-old democracy still holds, even if we can no longer deny its fragility. Neither the transition in leadership nor the first days of the Biden administration will be described by our historians as peaceful, but the ceremony will be remembered for its elegance and its literal and figurative colors worn by the guests of honor: suffragette white; Oshun yellow and Shango red in the African spiritual tradition; and of course, in the case of our vice president, Shirley Chisholm purple. The mosaic of American and world citizens watching on screens everywhere will be remembered for the

We have a lot we need to handle in the days ahead, but I know together we can get it done.
—**Kamala Harris**

pearls they wore around their necks and the Chuck Taylor sneakers on their feet. The scent of curry, collard greens, roast chicken, and Irish stew and the glasses of champagne and bottles of beer consumed by celebrants all over the world, especially in India, Jamaica, and California, celebrated a moment of movement forward for humanity that was almost stolen not only by the COVID-19 pandemic but by people whose American dream is characterized by authoritarianism and exclusion.

The hull of our country's ship continued to be battered by tsunamis of crisis, including the impeachment trial against the former president for inciting an insurrection. Though he was acquitted, he faces other legal challenges ahead.

We come from many places—the people and our leaders—by force and by our own will for reasons that are noble and its opposite. We have our sails tilted in a myriad of directions. We are all being carried by the waves of change with a government founded on an idea of a government "of the people, by the people, for the people" riding in the same American boat, now with Vice President Kamala Harris and President Joe Biden at the helm. ■

Part One

AN AMERICAN GIRL

October 20, 1964

Kamala Harris's story begins in a tumultuous time in modern America: the 1960s, when her parents, one from India, the other from Jamaica, each chose to immigrate to a country they'd never seen in order to pursue their graduate studies at the University of California, Berkeley. It was a time when America was digging deeper and deeper into an unwinnable foreign war in Vietnam. Because of television, a relatively new technology, civilian Americans witnessed the horrors of war for the first time from their own homes. The images they saw galvanized an unprecedented antiwar movement that intersected with the women's movement, the counterculture movement, and the mother of all modern American movements: the civil rights movement.

Harris's mother, Shyamala Gopalan, was nineteen when she graduated in 1957 from the University of Delhi's Lady Irwin College with the degree most common for women at that time: a BSc in Home Science. Determined to study advanced sciences, she applied and was admitted to a master's degree program in nutrition and endocrinology at the University of California, Berkeley. She arrived in the US in 1958. (She would earn her PhD in 1964 and build a brilliant career as a dedicated teacher and biomedical scientist conducting breast cancer research.)

Previous pages: Candidate Harris and a young supporter at a rally at Texas Southern University in Houston, March 23, 2019. **Opposite:** Kamala Harris with her mother, Shyamala Gopalan Harris, ca. 1965.

Harris's father, Donald Harris, a graduate of the University of the West Indies and the recipient of a prestigious government scholarship, immigrated in 1961 to pursue a doctorate in economics at Berkeley, which he received in 1965. (He would eventually serve as an economic advisor to his home country and become an esteemed professor of economics at Stanford University, where he is now a professor emeritus.)

As there were few foreign students at Berkeley at the time, they each looked beyond the campus to find people with whom they could share common concerns and ideas. Wearing a traditional Indian sari, Shyamala especially stood out, and she sought places where she could meet people who saw her as a peer and didn't gawk at her like an oddity. She and Donald were welcomed by a multicultural community that, while relatively small in number, was dynamic, particularly a group known as the Afro-American Association, which was started by a group of UC graduate and law students to educate African Americans about their history. That's where they met in 1962. It was a time when Berkeley on the whole was becoming, in the words of the *New York Times*, "a crucible of radical politics, as the trade-union left overlapped with early Black nationalist thinkers." Many of these thinkers came from the ranks of Black youth who were the descendants of enslaved people who migrated from the southeastern states.

> *My mother chose to pursue a marriage based on love, which is one of the greatest expressions of optimism that any one of us makes.*
> **—Kamala Harris**

The association would go on to make important contributions to the embryonic discipline of Black studies and to the creation of modern Black American rituals drawn from African traditions, such as the holiday Kwanzaa. Huey P. Newton and Bobby Seale, who cofounded the Black Panther Party in 1966, were in the mix. The main chapter of the national Black Panther Party was in Oakland.

Speakers were often asked to share their knowledge of other cultures. Donald was a speaker one evening about Jamaican life and politics; Shyamala was in the audience. In the exchange of ideas, Shyamala and Donald fell in love, and they married the next year. They were each twenty-four years old; he was her first boyfriend, and she would be, in Kamala Harris's words, "going against traditions in her family dating back to 500 BC, my mother chose to pursue a marriage based on love, which is one of the greatest expressions of optimism that any one of us makes."

The couple had Kamala, their first child, October 20, 1964, the year Shyamala earned her PhD and Martin Luther King Jr. received the Nobel Peace Prize. Kamala's sister, Maya, was born two years later. In between, Donald received his PhD in economics.

The Afro-Indian American girls grew up in a community of Black and brown people, in what they describe in their speeches, books, and interviews as an atmosphere of love and encouragement. Like most families in academia and the sciences, they were not rich, not poor, but cultured. Their household was punctuated with art—carvings from Africa and India, framed posters of work by Studio Museum in Harlem artists—and kept "ready for company with fresh-cut flowers."

A 2021 *Essence* article noted that meals at their dinner table "would run the gamut from collard greens to curries. Their faith melded Hindu and Baptist practices. Activists would come to dinner and strategize." Harris wrote in her autobiography, "My parents and their friends were more than just protesters. They were big thinkers, pushing big ideas, organizing their community." She often tells the story of how they brought her along in their activities, pushing her in a stroller on marches. She remembers "a sea of legs moving about, of the energy and shouts and chants. Social justice was a central part of family discussions." She'd grow restless, as children do, and would wiggle and whine. When she was asked, "What do you want?" Her response was, in toddler speak, "Fweedom."

The young family, a cross-cultural union, became a part of the cultural fabric in the Bay Area and formed a bridge of relationships to their extended families in India and Jamaica. Their parents took the girls on visits to both places and gave them an understanding of their ancestral

Above: Kamala Harris's parents, Shyamala Gopalan and Donald Harris.

ties. The marriage, though, began to strain. Kamala writes in her memoir *The Truths We Hold* (2019) that she imagines things might have turned out better had they not been so young. The couple separated, then divorced in 1972, when she was eight years old. After that, she writes, "We would see [my father] on weekends and spend the summers with him in Palo Alto. But it was really my mother who took charge of our upbringing."

About a year after her parents separated, Shyamala moved with her daughters to the Flatlands, a working-class part of Berkeley with a significant African American population. "Everyone in the neighborhood knew us as 'Shyamala and the girls,'" she recalled. She described the neighborhood as having "a richness of conscience. People looked out for each other. Neighbors cared about what was going on up and down the block. And safety was a community value."

Kamala attended a local Montessori school for kindergarten, and then, beginning in first grade, was bused from the Flatlands to a prosperous white neighborhood to attend Thousand Oaks Elementary School. "I only learned later that we were part of a national experiment in desegregation," she wrote in her book, while reflecting on "how wonderful it was to grow up in such a diverse environment."

> *How wonderful it was to grow up in such a diverse environment.*
> **—Kamala Harris**

On Sundays, Shyamala sent the girls to the 23rd Avenue Church of God, where they sang in the children's choir. Kamala's favorite hymn was "Fill My Cup, Lord." She was a regular girl whose heroes were her first grade teacher, Mrs. Wilson, and her best friends, who loved dance class at Madame Bovie's ballet studio. Some of her friends from kindergarten, such as Stacey Johnson-Batiste, remain in her circle of friends to this day.

Harris writes in her memoir that her favorite day of the week was Thursday, when they went to what she describes as "an unassuming beige building at the corner of what was then Grove Street and Derby. Once a mortuary, the building I knew was bursting with life, home to a pioneering black cultural center." The place was called the Rainbow Sign. It served as a movie house, performance space, lecture hall, art gallery, and restaurant—a safe place to discuss current events and a place

Opposite: Kamala Harris with her father, Donald Harris, April 1965.

where cultural icons like Maya Angelou, James Baldwin, and Huey P. Newton casually dropped in.

The Rainbow Sign was an example of how minorities were obliged to create safe spaces to be themselves and find safety in numbers wherever they could. The mainstream or dominant culture in America had not internalized its own message that all humans are equal and endowed with inalienable rights. And even children such as Kamala and Maya could see that harsh truth. "My mother was the strongest person I have ever known," Harris wrote in her memoir. "But I also knew my mother was a target. I saw it, and it made me mad. . . . [M]y brilliant mother being treated as though she were dumb because of her accent. Memories of her being followed around a department store with suspicion," because she was "a brown-skinned woman."

MONTREAL, CANADA

Kamala was twelve when her mother accepted a teaching and research position in Montreal at McGill University and the affiliated Jewish General Hospital, where she could conduct breast cancer research. The preteen was not keen to leave sunny California for the mostly French-speaking, wintry Quebec province in February 1977 in the middle of the school year, but Shyamala encouraged her daughters to think of it as an adventure. During the five years they spent in Canada, the sisters satisfied some of their yearning for their hometown by returning for visits during holidays and the summer break, staying either with their father or with Regina Shelton, who had been like a second mother to them growing up.

In Montreal, Kamala's education had a rocky start at first. Shyamala had enrolled her in a French-speaking primary school so she could learn the language, even though Kamala knew only a few French words from her ballet classes. Shyamala eventually relented to her daughter's pleas to switch schools, and Kamala happily finished eighth grade at the bilingual Fine Arts Core Elementary, many of whose graduates have done things related to music, theater, politics, social themes, or community. For high school, she went to Westmount High, the oldest English-speaking and one of the most diverse public schools in Quebec with a population then of 60 percent white and 40 percent Black students. As reported in

the *New York Times*, "Her childhood friends recalled a confident young woman who showed seeds of activism, found cultural affirmation in her Black identity and complained about French class."

After Kamala's high school graduation in 1981, the family returned to the Bay area. Kamala and Maya were expected to pursue higher education, and the young women themselves aspired to earn advanced degrees. "During high school, I started thinking more concretely about my future—college and beyond. I'd always assumed I would have a career; I'd seen the satisfaction my parents derived from their work," Kamala wrote. Her father was a college professor, and her mother was doing remarkable work on the efforts to cure breast cancer. "When I was a kid, I used to accompany my mother to the lab, where she'd give me jobs to do. Cleaning test tubes, mainly. I think she probably knew early on that I wasn't going to follow her into the sciences. It was the humanities and the arts that spoke to me, even as I was in awe of my mother and her colleagues and their work."

It was time for Kamala to decide which college she would attend. ■

Above: Kamala Harris at her mother's lab in Berkeley, California, in the mid-1970s.

Influences

ROOTS: INDIA & JAMAICA

Kamala Harris once described India as a place where "one of the highest callings . . . is to be a studied and learned person." Her mother, Shyamala Gopalan, was the oldest child in a high-achieving family that immigrated in 1958 to a land she knew little about and had never before visited.

This was an era when higher education was not a common expectation for a girl, even if the family could afford it. But Shyamala's family was a bit different from most in their social group in India, a society based on a caste system. As a teenager, she left home with the blessing of her parents, but not without a negotiation on the terms. Kamala Harris writes in her memoir, *The Truths We Hold,* that her mother "had cut a deal with her parents. When her studies were complete, she was supposed to return home to India where the plan was for her to settle down into a long-arranged marriage." Needless to say, Shyamala didn't keep up her end of the bargain.

The Gopalans are Tamil Brahmins, who have been the highest caste of priests and Hindu scholars in the southern Indian region of Tamil Nadu for nearly two thousand years. Under British rule, the Tamil Brahmins were positioned as administrators and government officials, and they continued to serve as government leaders, university professors, jurists, and scientists up to modern times.

The homeplace of Kamala Harris's clan is Madras, now called Chennai, the capital of Tamil Nadu. Harris writes in her book that her mother was raised "in a household where political activism and civic leadership came naturally. . . . She was born with a sense of justice imprinted on her soul." Her grandmother, Rajam Gopalan, was "a skilled community organizer" and her grandfather, P. V. Gopalan, "had been part of the movement to win India's Independence." When Kamala was still very small, her grandfather took her by

Her grandmother, Rajam Gopalan, was "a skilled community organizer" and her grandfather, P. V. Gopalan, "had been part of the movement to win India's independence."

Opposite: Villagers in and around Thulasendrapuram, India—Kamala Harris's grandfather's hometown—set off firecrackers, carried posters, and offered prayers in celebration of her victory, November 8, 2020.

the hand on his daily walks, and she listened as he talked to his friends about the events of the day. Harris cites these early conversations with her grandfather as an important introduction to what would become her world of politics and concerns for social justice.

––––––––––

Like her mother, Kamala Harris's father, Donald Harris, comes from a country shaped by a long history of British rule and political and social ferment, and a tradition of intellectualism and scholarship. Jamaica, one of the largest of the Caribbean islands and home to the native Taíno and Arawak people, was seized by the Spanish in 1509 and by the British in 1655, and it would only finally win independence in 1962. Under British rule, Jamaica became a highly lucrative colony of sugar plantations, thanks to the enslaved labor of as many as a million Africans who were kidnapped and trafficked across the Atlantic.

After slavery ended in Jamaica in 1834, more than a half million Indians were shipped to the Caribbean islands to work the sugar plantations as indentured servants. Donald Harris, born in 1938, the same year as Shyamala, is said to be a direct descendant of Hamilton Brown, the Irish-born British owner of a plantation in Saint Ann Parish, now named Brown's Town, where Harris's family resided.

In recent generations, Harris family members have run for local office and have been community organizers and business owners. The family is also known for their philanthropic efforts.

When Donald's grandmother, Iris Finegan, and his parents, Beryl and Oscar Harris, met their son's bride, with her brown skin and flowing black hair, they would have seen a familiar, albeit, new face. The *Gleaner*, a Jamaican newspaper notes that "Harris comes from a stock of high achievers" on both sides of her family. In recent generations, Harris family members have run for local office and have been community organizers and business owners. The family is also known for their philanthropic efforts.

While most academically ambitious Jamaicans traveled to England for their education, Donald Harris had different ideas. Growing up in Jamaica, Donald listened to jazz broadcast from Nashville's WLAC and also from the military base at Guantánamo Bay, Cuba, and he was drawn to the country that produced those sounds. When Harris won a scholarship to study abroad, he spurned Europe and instead set his sights on the University of California, Berkeley. According to the *New York Times*, Harris had read about student activists from Berkeley campaigning for civil rights in the South and decided that this was the university he would attend.

It was American jazz and student protest that brought Donald Harris to pursue his graduate studies in economics to California in 1962, where he would meet and one year later marry an intense PhD biomedical student from India. ■

Harris in Jamaica with her great-grandmother
Iris Finegan, aka Miss Iris, in 1966.

JAN • 70 •

"*For a long time, this was my tiny little family: my mom, my grandma, and my aunt. I joke that my household was like the opening scene of the* Wonder Woman *movie, where brilliant women run around an all-female island helping each other succeed.*"

—Meena Harris, Kamala Harris's niece

Opposite: Kamala Harris (left) with her younger sister, Maya, and mother, Shyamala, outside their apartment on Milvia Street in Berkeley in January 1970.
Above: Kamala Harris with her sister, Maya (Meena's mother), Christmas 1968.

> *There was a richness of conscience.*
> *People looked out for each other.*
> *Neighbors cared about what was*
> *going on up and down the block.*
>
> **—Kamala Harris**

Opposite: Grade school students board a school bus in February 1970, eighteen months after Berkeley's controversial desegregation program began. **Above:** Kamala Harris (standing in red skirt) and her sister, Maya (in chair), attend neighbor Yalda Uhls's (front left wearing crown) backyard birthday party in 1971.

Influences

THE RAINBOW SIGN

Cultural centers sprang up in Black communities all over the country in the 1960s and 1970s. They answered the growing thirst among Black people to freely express themselves in civic and cultural ways. They were a safe place in a climate of political ferment and racial terrorism to sort out the issues that concerned them.

Despite the geographical distance between the regions of the country, the Great Migration and other mass Black movements bonded African Americans—notwithstanding class divisions and differences in backgrounds—across regions. It was not so unusual for famous people to march along with and perform for the benefit of the rank and file, "the people."

The Rainbow Sign, a Black cultural center in Berkeley, California, was founded as a place for the "total exposition of the Black cultural experience," as the local news station KRON reported. It was "a hub for black art, music, cinema, literature, education and civic gathering— that drew cultural icons from across the country from Maya Angelou and James Baldwin to Nina Simone and Huey P. Newton" of the Black Panther Party (which had its base in Oakland).

The center displayed the art of now world-renowned and iconic artists, including Elizabeth Catlett, Kofi Bailey, and Samella Lewis. The organization often struggled financially and worked hard to keep the lights on more than anything. But on any given day, according to a history of the center hosted on UC Berkeley's website, you might find people from "a Jewish organization or Oakland's Black Muslim Bakery—streaming into a meeting in the club's rentable conference room. Over it all would waft the aroma of soul food, served seven days a week from the on-site restaurant. Amid the clink of dishes in the program hall, there would be the clamor of concert preparations—tables and chairs being moved to make way for microphone stands and drum sets. And bustling throughout would be a dynamic woman in a bold-patterned dress— the charismatic [executive director] Mary Ann Pollar—smiling, smoking, and orchestrating her vision." ∎

Left: Mary Ann Pollar, founder and executive director of the Rainbow Sign, ca. 1974.
Opposite: Contact sheet of James Baldwin's visit to the Rainbow Sign in 1976. The novelist was a longtime friend of Mary Ann Pollar (seen wearing a headband and patterned dress) and a frequent guest at the cultural center.

Speech

BREAK SOME RULES

Commencement Address, San Francisco State University, May 26, 2007

President Corrigan, distinguished faculty, families and friends, and of course you, the members of the class of 2007, I'm so pleased to say "You did it!"

And I know it was a team effort, including your family and your friends and of course Facebook and Red Bull and PS3s.

And I know today is the kind of day where I should talk about where you are going. But first, I'd like to spend a few moments talking about where you've been. This spring, one and a half million students will sit in ceremonies much like this at thousands of universities and colleges across the country. But I can assure you from where I stand, very few of those ceremonies will look like yours.

After all, this is San Francisco, a city where one hundred different languages are spoken, where one-third of us were born in another country, and where many more of our parents, like mine, were born in another country. And you, San Francisco State graduates, are just as diverse and energetic as the city itself. This is the city and the school that has produced countless leaders and activists.

These are people who broke barriers, people whose names we know because they broke barriers—and in many different ways by perse-

vering, working hard, and achieving your goal of graduation, you have broken barriers. And there are many more barriers you will face and break—and must face and break—to achieve your dreams.

So I want to talk to you today about that, about breaking barriers to achieve your dreams and our dreams for your future. And it's more than a notion. To do it, you may have to break some rules. And I'm not talking about the kind of rules that I prosecute, so don't get any ideas. But I am talking about the old rules and ways of thinking about who can lead, what they look like, who their family is, and what neighborhoods they're from. I'm also talking about the barriers of belief that suggest that things cannot be changed and that problems cannot be solved.

When you graduates break all of these barriers, you will open up new possibilities and create new solutions to our challenges. You will become the new leaders with new perspectives and a new way of thinking about how to create solutions that no one thought possible.

And let me tell you, by definition, breaking barriers will take you on paths that you never thought imaginable.

Frankly, that's what happened to me.

Above: Shyamala Gopalan (left) with her friend Lenore Pomerance at a civil rights protest in Berkeley, California in the 1960s.

I faced a barrier of traditional thinking about how to be a fighter for civil rights. When I was growing up, as President Corrigan said, my parents were deeply involved in the civil rights movement in the seventies in Berkeley, and I grew up surrounded by people who were constantly marching and shouting at the top of their lungs for equality and for justice. And of course, I was right there marching with them, in a stroller, but I was there and marching for the justice that needed to exist and should be demanded.

By the time I got to Howard University, I wanted to continue that fight. And the traditional thinking was that you could only do civil rights work in organizations such as the ACLU or the NAACP. The thinking was that you had to work from the outside in, but I believed it was important to be at the table where decisions and important decisions were being made, and that's why I decided to become a prosecutor. And yes, it was about the farthest thing from my parents' mind, so you can imagine when I told them that I was going to be a member of law enforcement, I pretty much had to defend the decision like a thesis.

But they understood.

You see, their march for civil rights led me on a path to a courtroom where I stood before a jury of twelve people arguing for justice for an abused child, arguing for justice for a battered spouse, arguing for justice for a victim of hate crime. And following that passion for civil rights has been the greatest reward of my career.

As you grow in your career, you'll experience similar barriers of traditional thinking and also other barriers—for example, the limits that others set for you, barriers that place a ceiling on what you can accomplish and who you can be.

I know you will have the creativity and the independence to say yes where others have said no; where others have seen risk, to see opportunity; and where others have felt fear, to find courage.

And I've been there, too. When I decided to run for district attorney, it was considered a man's job, even here in San Francisco. No woman had ever been elected district attorney in San Francisco; no person of color had ever been elected district attorney of San Francisco.

And I remember the day that I got my first poll results. I was sitting in a small conference room and a little nervous, but also hopeful, and then I read them. I was at 6 percent in the polls. And you can imagine that didn't feel good. In fact, I felt pretty small. And then I was told what you have all probably heard at some point in your life and will certainly hear in your future. I was told that I should wait my turn. I was told, "Don't put yourself through all of that." I was told that I should give up. I was told that I had no chance.

And I didn't listen.

And I'm telling you: Don't you listen, either. Don't you dare listen when they try to tell you you can't do it, or it hasn't been done before. I know that every one of you here has quietly and privately thought and believes that you can do something great. Nurture and cherish that belief. Own that vision.

And surround yourself with people who will support you and will encourage your ambition. And don't listen when people say it hasn't been done before.

Armed with the belief in yourself and surrounded by those who believe in you, I know you will have the creativity and the independence to say yes where others have said no; where others have seen risk, to see opportunity; and where others have felt fear, to find courage.

And it's an extraordinary time in which to graduate. Consider how we can now break barriers and create new possibilities. Right now in our city and our country, we are facing enormous social, political, and economic challenges. For example, our civil liberties are under fire, and our federal government is not just failing to enforce them but is frankly contributing to their deterioration.

And we can stand against that with passion and conviction.

In politics, for the first time, barriers are being broken by men and women from every walk of life. Just think: For the first time ever, three of the strongest candidates for president of the United States are a woman, a Latino, and an African American. And we can elect a new kind of president.

Across the world, new frontiers in civil rights are emerging as the forces of globalization connect our lives in real time with citizens of every country, rich and poor. We can be the ones to fight for human rights and stop the genocide in Darfur. And we have a growing environmental crisis around the world. Our air, our water, our oceans—we can be the ones to protect them. We can be the ones to find new solutions. And here in San Francisco, there are over 2,400 children who have been designated as chronically truant from our schools. Over seven hundred of them are elementary school students. We can be the ones to mentor them. We can be the ones to make sure that we get them in school. We can make sure that in ten years, they are sitting where you are sitting today. In times like these, it is dangerous to stay quiet and stay on the sidelines. Times like

these call for people like you to stand up, to be inspired, and to act inspired. To break barriers, to drive change, and to roll up your sleeves instead of throwing up your hands.

So I ask you, who's going to stand up and defend a woman's right to reproductive freedom? Who's going to ensure that environmental justice occurs so we stop dumping and polluting in our poorest neighborhoods and communities of color? Who is going to speak up against the torture in Guantanamo Bay?

In politics, for the first time, barriers are being broken by men and women from every walk of life. Just think: For the first time ever, three of the strongest candidates for president of the United States are a woman, a Latino, and an African American. And we can elect a new kind of president.

And who is going to register people to vote and work on a campaign and help us elect a president who will end the war in Iraq? The answer is that you, you, you graduates of 2007 will be at the heart of these great struggles. So follow your passion, eat your Wheaties, and get on out there, because today you graduate, and tomorrow there is no barrier on what you can do. ■

KAMALA HARRIS
Cher Mem: California,
Angelo; summer '80;
I Rem: "S"ing out the "W"
with AC, DP, CS, MM,
Happ Is: Making long distance
phone calls to A.M.
Fav Past: Dancing with super
six; Midnight Magic
Fav Ex: Naw, I'm just playing!
Sp Thks to: My mother
Part Note: Be cool MA YA!

Kamala Harris during her time at Westmount High School in
Montreal, Canada (top photo: second from left; opposite photo:
front row center in tan jacket). Images are from the Westmount
High School yearbook in 1981, the year she graduated.

1981

Part Two

A PURSUIT OF JUSTICE

Who Are We?

As Kamala Harris wrote in her memoir, "Though the seed was planted early on, I'm not sure when, exactly, I wanted to be a lawyer." She recalled, "Some of my greatest heroes were lawyers: Thurgood Marshall, Charles Hamilton Houston, and Constance Baker Motley—giants of the civil rights movement. I cared a lot about fairness, and I saw the law as a tool that can make things fair."

Kamala had a fine set of educational institutions to choose from right in her backyard, including the alma mater of both of her parents, the University of California, Berkeley. Family friends, though, sang the praises of attending one of the HBCUs—historically Black colleges and universities. Her aunt Chris, in particular, had talked to Kamala about her alma mater, Howard University, the oldest of the HBCUs, saying it was "a wonderful place" and "an institution with an extraordinary legacy." Kamala chose Howard. "I wanted to get off on the right foot. And what better place to do this, I thought, than at Thurgood Marshall's alma mater."

In the late summer of 1982, when she was not yet eighteen, she moved across the country to Washington, DC, thousands of miles from home. The nation's capital was home to a large population of Black people—many of them the descendants of the enslaved people who built the White House, and others who settled there from the African diaspora. The vibe of this urban metropolis on the Potomac—with its

Previous pages: Senator Cory Booker of New Jersey looks on while Senator Kamala Harris questions US Supreme Court nominee Brett Kavanaugh at his confirmation hearing, September 2018. **Opposite:** Alameda County deputy district attorney Kamala Harris, 1997.

vibrant music, arts, culture, and politics scene—was so Black it was called "Chocolate City."

In her memoir, Kamala recalls how she felt when she first arrived at Howard: "I'll always remember walking into Cramton Auditorium for my freshman orientation. The room was packed. I stood in the back, looked around, and thought, 'This is heaven!' There were hundreds of people and they all looked like me." Like many Black youth of the first generation bused to attend newly desegregated schools, going to a school with a Black majority meant an end to isolation. Robin Givhan of the *Washington Post* wrote, "Howard was a place that allowed for the vastness of the Black experience. Whether it be the first generation college-goer

from a small town in the South or the scion of a family of professionals from Chicago or a wealthy international student from Ghana. The idea that Blackness could be many things—none of which required an apology or dilution—was a core tenet of Howard and one that speaks to the essence of Harris herself."

"I dove [into Howard] with gusto." Kamala recalls in her memoir. "Freshman year, I ran for my first elected office: freshman class representative of the Liberal Arts Student Council." She chaired the Economics Society and competed on the debate team. She participated in a long-held tradition among aspiring Black Americans in their college experience, pledging Alpha Kappa Alpha (AKA) sorority, one of the nine Black Greek letter organizations (BLGO), known as the Divine Nine. She wore the pink and green colors that are a part of her sorority's group identity, went to parties, learned their signature dance moves, and participated in the step shows that have become a hallmark of Black coed social life.

She did not fall into the trap of all play and no work, however. Not Shyamala's child. Her mother raised her daughters to value all kinds of work. In her book, Kamala recalled times when her mother would come

Above: Howard University's namesake and cofounder, Union general Oliver Otis Howard, ca. 1865. **Opposite:** Howard University in Washington, DC, was chartered on March 2, 1867, as "a University for the education of youth in the liberal arts and sciences."

home from a good day at work with flowers to give to their babysitter, saying to her, "'I wouldn't have been able to do what I did if you didn't do what you do. . . . Thank you for everything.'"

While at Howard, Kamala held a number of outside jobs. She interned at the Federal Trade Commission, did research at the National Archives, and was a tour guide at the US Bureau of Engraving and Printing. She also secured an internship with Senator Alan Cranston of California. "I loved going to the Capitol Building every day that summer for work. It felt like the epicenter of change—even as an intern sorting mail." Maybe that was when the seeds of her future began to sprout. Thirty years later, she would enter the same building, not as an intern, but as a US senator.

She earned her bachelor of arts degree in political science and economics in 1986. She is a proud alumna of Howard, which has produced a multitude of Black leaders in a wide range of fields with, as she put it to Howard graduates when she was the guest commencement speaker in 2017, "a legacy that has now endured and thrived for 150 years."

THE LAW

After graduation, Kamala enrolled in the University of California Hastings College of the Law. Raised by activists and critical thinkers who might have expected her to work outside government and the systems that tended to hurt more than help marginal communities, she decided to work in law enforcement as a prosecutor. She said that in telling her family about her decision, "I pretty much had to defend the decision like a thesis."

She was optimistic that she could successfully fight for the well-being and security of people from inside the system. Law school was where she says she "made the obvious connection between civil rights and public safety. I noticed when we file a criminal complaint, we don't write the name of the victim versus the name of the defendant. We write 'The People' versus the defendant." "The People" included those at the top of society and those at the bottom.

In her second year at Hastings, she landed an internship at the Alameda County district attorney's office. Her office was once headed by chief justice of the Supreme Court Earl Warren, who wrote the majority

opinion in *Brown v. Board of Education*. This was the court decision that ended the idea that "separate but equal" was justice and affirmed that *all* citizens, including African Americans, are entitled to equality, period. The internship led to her first job as a lawyer after her graduation in 1989. For the next eight years, she worked as a deputy district attorney in Alameda, where she found her niche in prosecuting child sexual assault cases, homicides, and robbery—tough cases of violent crime. In 1998, she joined the San Francisco district attorney's office, ultimately becoming managing attorney of the Career Criminal Unit and then head of its Division on Children and Families. She explained, "I was going to do the [prosecutor] job through the lens of my own experiences and perspectives, from wisdom gained at my mother's knee . . . and on the Howard Yard."

IRONING-BOARD POLITICS

Harris soon came to realize that while her job enabled her to effect positive change in the way laws in her state were enforced, to be even more effective, she needed to sit at the tables where policy decisions were being

Above: Kamala Harris and Gwen Whitfield at an anti-apartheid protest while attending Howard University, 1982.

made. She decided to jump into the fray of elected leadership, and in 2002, she prepared to run for the office of district attorney. She was well aware that all San Francisco district attorneys since the first one in 1856 had been white and male. She might have heard the voice of her father, how he took her and her sister on long hikes and encouraged her not to be afraid, to "run!"

Against conventional advice, Harris located her campaign in Bayview, one of the communities characterized by the marginal poor, immigrants, and homeless people. San Francisco, while ethnically diverse, was and remains mostly segregated by race and class. "I wasn't running so I could have a fancy office downtown. I was running for the chance to represent people whose voices weren't being heard, and to bring the promise of public safety to every neighborhood, not just some." She proved the naysayers wrong.

"My mother often took charge of the volunteer operation, and she didn't dillydally. Everyone [on her campaign team] knew that when Shyamala spoke, you listened." Shyamala made sure the small but important things were taken care of, like having duct tape and an ironing board to set up as a standing desk at campaign stops to hold clipboards and brochures to hand out to volunteers and would-be voters.

Dozens of supporters showed up for her in Bayview. "Our campaign attracted people representing the full vibrancy of the whole community. Volunteers and supporters poured in from Chinatown, the Castro, Pacific Heights, the Mission District: white, black, Asian, and Latinx; wealthy and working-class; male and female; old and young; gay and straight." Harris positioned herself as a "'get-it-done' progressive."

She was challenged to walk a narrow gauntlet. "There was no such thing as 'a progressive prosecutor,'" said *Mother Jones* writer Jamilah King in an interview about Harris's entry into statewide politics. "Coming into the '80s and '90s, there was still a lot of 'tough on crime' rhetoric that politicians needed to use to get elected."

Kamala's victory in 2004 against the incumbent in a close, hotly contested race broke through a major glass ceiling. She became the first woman, first African American, and first South Asian district attorney in San Francisco's history and, at the same time, the first to hold such an office in the entire state of California. (She would be elected for a subsequent term.)

Once she was the DA, she was able to launch such progressive initiatives as Back on Track, a program that offered an alternative to incarceration for first-time nonviolent offenders. Instead of being sent to prison, participants were committed to a twelve-to-eighteen-month reentry program involving every important aspect of their lives, including employment, education, and parenting. The pilot program proved its merit within two years, inspired the creation of others, and was eventually adopted as a model program by the Obama Justice Department.

She also challenged another industry of institutions where systemic discrimination played out: housing. She took a leading role in creating a mortgage fraud unit to make up for what the federal government was failing to do for homeowners subject to unfair mortgage terms and treatment by banks.

Kamala's work as San Francisco's DA was rewarding and challenging, but nothing like the challenge she faced in her personal life. In February 2008, her beloved mother scheduled a special dinner out for Kamala and her sister Maya, who was there on a visit from New York City, where she was living and working as an attorney with the Ford Foundation. Shyamala gave her daughters the news that she'd been diagnosed with colon cancer. They rearranged their lives to be with their mother as much as possible, especially when she was undergoing chemotherapy and other treatments. At the same time, encouraged by her mother and sister, Kamala continued preparations to enter the statewide race for attorney general. After almost two terms as district attorney, she wanted to be in a position to effect change beyond San Francisco. Kamala's work provided a place to productively channel her energy and pain.

After she announced her campaign, one longtime political strategist publicly commented that she could not win. "A woman running for attorney general, a woman who is a minority, a woman who is a minority . . . who is anti–death penalty, who is DA of wacky San Francisco." Kamala's response: "Old stereotypes die hard. I was convinced that my perspective and experience made me the strongest candidate in the race."

Even as she was going through the paces of cancer treatment, Shyamala kept up with her daughter's campaign. When Kamala said to her, "Mommy, these guys are saying they're gonna kick my ass," her mother laughed even through her discomfort, a knowing laugh that said the opposition clearly didn't know how tough the Harris women are. As Kamala herself has said, "When you break through a glass ceiling, you're going to get cut."

Shyamala Gopalan Harris, the world-renowned biomedical scientist, teacher, and breast cancer researcher who Kamala Harris credits as the most important influence in her life, lost her battle against cancer on February 11, 2009. She was seventy years old. While grieving her greatest personal loss, Kamala crisscrossed the state campaigning for the post that, if she won, would make her the first female and first African American attorney general for the state of California. The 2010 election was hard fought and the ballot counting continued for twenty-one days after the polls closed. Kamala won by a margin of less than 1 percent. She would be reelected to a second term four years later.

But before that next election, Doug Emhoff would come into her life.

The couple met in 2013 on a blind date arranged by her longtime best friend Chrisette Hudlin. She and her filmmaker husband, Reginald, had been impressed by attorney Douglas Emhoff during a business meeting in Los Angeles. He was amicably divorced, the father of a grown son and daughter, Jewish, born and raised in New Jersey, and a partner in a firm specializing in entertainment and intellectual property law. Kamala was single and in her forties, a Black professional in a high-powered political job and very much in the public eye. Chrisette knew that dating wasn't easy for her friend, to put it mildly. She gave Kamala's phone number to Doug and persuaded her to take his call. They hit it off from the start. It didn't take long for him to introduce her to his children or for her to let him see her at work and meet her extended family, because they soon figured out that they were compatible despite—and maybe because—of their distinct accomplishments and varied backgrounds. They had their San Francisco courthouse wedding on August 22, 2014. Maya Harris officiated and read from the work of the celebrated writer Maya Angelou (whom the sisters had met at the Rainbow Sign when they were youngsters).

The ceremony blended cultural rituals: Kamala placed a garland of flowers around Doug's neck in the Indian tradition, and he stepped on a glass at the end of the ceremony in the Jewish tradition. In the classic American tradition, the couple make a habit of gathering together with family and friends for Sunday dinner, home-cooked by Momala. That's what her stepchildren, Ella and Cole, call her—*stepmother* doesn't have the right vibe for them.

Five months later, her career would take a turn once again when Barbara Boxer announced in early January 2015 that she would retire at the end of her fourth term as US senator. It created the first open Senate seat in California in twenty-four years. Kamala couldn't pass on the opportunity to become a US senator, knowing that the position would enable her to take the issues she cared about to the national level. She announced her candidacy on January 13, 2015, almost two years before the 2016 election.

On November 8, 2016, Kamala won with more than 60 percent of the vote, setting another precedent.

California had never before in its history elected a Black, Latino, or Asian politician to the US Senate. She would also become only the second Black woman elected to the US Senate in the nation's history; Carol Moseley Braun of Illinois broke that barrier in 1993 and served one term.

Kamala Harris of California served as senator in the 115th and 116th US Congresses during the final weeks of Barack Obama's presidency and throughout Donald Trump's term. She voiced concerns and opinions at many committee meetings and public hearings; her debate skills and experience as a prosecutor were much in evidence. Not surprisingly, pro-Harris political action groups formed, among other supporters, to promote her as a candidate for president. When she made the decision to run for the office, she said, "This is a moment in time where I feel a sense of responsibility to stand up and fight for the best of who we are." ■

> *Family means everything to me. I've had many titles throughout my career, but Momala will always be the one that means the most to me.*
>
> —Kamala Harris

Economics

> *The campus was a place where you didn't have to be confined to the box of another person's choosing. At Howard, you could come as you were and leave as the person you aspired to be.*
>
> **—Kamala Harris**

Above: Howard University student Kamala Harris (back row center) posing with the Economics Club for the yearbook. **Opposite:** Kamala Harris's yearbook graduation photo, Howard University class of 1986.

Influences

LIFTING UP AND GIVING BACK

Historically Black Colleges and Universities

Literacy was understood by slaveholders as a tool that Blacks could use against them. Throughout the antebellum South, especially after Nat Turner's antislavery rebellion in 1831, laws prohibited teaching an enslaved person to read and write, and those who learned and were discovered were punished. Even before slavery ended, though, Black people took every opportunity they could to educate themselves.

The first school established for the higher education of Black people was the African Institute, founded in 1837 in Philadelphia by a white Quaker and later renamed the Institute for Colored Youth. The Ashmun Institute, also in Philadelphia, was established in 1854 (it was renamed Lincoln University in 1866 to honor the recently assassinated president), followed by Howard University in 1867, now perhaps the most renowned and prestigious of the historically Black colleges and universities.

Many more Black colleges were founded in the last quarter of the nineteenth century, including the Hampton Institute (Virginia; now Hampton University), Fisk University (Nashville), Meharry Medical College (Nashville), as well as Atlanta University Center's Morehouse, Spelman, Clark/Atlanta, and Morris Brown.

Today there are a little over one hundred private and public historically Black colleges and universities, known collectively as HBCUs. Graduates of HBCUs include singer-songwriter-producer Lionel Ritchie (Tuskegee Institute), media mogul and philanthropist Oprah Winfrey (Tennessee State University), and film director

Portrait of US Supreme Court justice Thurgood Marshall, 1967.

Spike Lee (Morehouse). Howard University alumni include the writers Zora Neale Hurston, Isabel Wilkerson, Ta-Nehisi Coates, and Toni Morrison; entertainment mogul and artist Sean Combs; former Atlanta mayor Shirley Franklin; Newark mayor Ras Baraka; and the late congressmen John Lewis and Elijah Cummings.

THE DIVINE NINE

If you've ever heard Vice President Harris greet an audience with the peculiar sound "Skee-Wee," know that she was issuing a familiar call to her beloved Sisterhood of the Ivy, her sorority sisters in Alpha Kappa Alpha.

At the HBCUs, African Americans found it necessary to create social networks and cultural practices to support their own—hence the creation of Black fraternities and sororities, the National Pan-Hellenic Council, or what is affectionately called the Divine Nine: the fraternities Alpha Phi Alpha, Kappa Alpha Psi, Omega Psi Phi, and Phi Beta Sigma, and the sororities Alpha Kappa Alpha, Delta Sigma Theta, Zeta Phi Beta, Iota Phi Theta, and Sigma Gamma Rho.

Kamala's sorority, Alpha Kappa Alpha, was founded at Howard in 1908. AKA has more than 1,000 chapters and 300,000 members across the world. Among its well-known members are the mathematicians Katherine Johnson, Dorothy Vaughan, and Mary Jackson, the women made famous for their work with NASA in the film *Hidden Figures*.

Philanthropy has always been a significant component of the mission of Black Greek-letter organizations; they give back to their communities by investing in scholarships, raising funds for the needy, and engaging in many other charitable activities. They also provide a network of support as their members navigate their personal and professional lives. When Kamala Harris became the vice presidential nominee, her AKA sisters found a distinctive way to show their support. Democratic fundraisers for Biden and Harris noticed something unusual about the contributions flowing into the campaign: Many were for exactly $19.08. Members of AKA were donating that specific amount to honor their connection to their sorority, which was founded in 1908. The Biden Victory Fund received more than 11,000 of these donations, totaling nearly $219,000. ∎

> **Family is my beloved Alpha Kappa Alpha, our Divine Nine, and my HBCU brothers and sisters.**
>
> **—Kamala Harris**

Opposite: Founding members of the Rho Chapter of Alpha Kappa Alpha Sorority, University of California, Berkeley, in 1921: (left to right) Virginia Stephens, Oreatheal Richardson, Myrtle Price (in back), Ida Jackson (sorority president), Talma Brooks, and Ruby Jefferson. **Above:** Senator Kamala Harris and fellow Alpha Kappa Alpha Sorority sisters singing the sorority's hymn at the annual Pink Ice Gala fundraiser in Columbia, South Carolina, January 25, 2019.

THE ROLE MODEL CLUB

Commencement Address, Howard University, May 13, 2017

Greetings, Bisons! It is so great to be back home. President Frederick, members of the board, distinguished faculty—thank you for this incredible honor. And to the class of 2017—congratulations! And to your families and friends who encouraged you and held you up—thank you for all you did. Let's hear it for them!

I've had the honor of speaking at many commencements. But this one is particularly special for me. Because decades ago, I sat just where you sit now, feeling the embrace of my Howard family. Our Howard family.

And a family, at its best, shares common values and aspirations. A family shares hardships and a connected history. A family looks for ways to support and inspire one another. Our family includes a young woman who worked her way through school and is graduating as a published poet—Angel Dye. It includes the fourth Rhodes Scholar in Howard's history—Cameron Clarke. It includes a woman who got elected to an advisory neighborhood commission at eighteen years old, the youngest elected official in DC history, and she is your HUSA president—Allyson Carpenter.

And our family also includes those who came before you. Thurgood Marshall and Zora Neale Hurston. Shirley Franklin and Doctor LaSalle Leffall. Mr. Vernon Jordan and Ta-Nehisi Coates. Elijah Cummings and Mayor Kasim Reed. And now, graduates, you are ready to join the ranks.

You are finally at your commencement. So look around. Capture this moment. Hold it in your heart, and hold it in your mind. You're looking at people you will read about for the trailblazing work they will do. You're looking at the faces of friends who one day will ask you to godparent their children. You may even be looking at someone you'll grow your family with—even if one or both of you doesn't fully know that right now. And graduates, also look back on the experiences you've already had.

Remember those first days on the Yard. Moving into the Quad and Drew. Learning how to navigate the Howard Runaround so you could get that dorm room or sign up for a class. Remember—or maybe even try to forget—all those late nights at Founders and those other nights at the Punchout or El Rey. Above all, remember that you are blessed. Wherever you came from, you now have the gift—the great gift—of a Howard University education.

And you are also part of a legacy that has now endured and thrived for 150 years. Endured when the doors of higher education were closed to Black students. Endured when segregation and discrimination were the law of the land. Endured when few recognized the potential and capacity of young Black men and women to be leaders.

But over the last 150 years, Howard has endured and thrived. Generations of students have been nurtured and challenged here—and provided with the tools and confidence to soar. Since this school was founded in 1867, Howard has awarded more than 120,000 degrees. It has prepared and produced thousands of Black lawyers and doctors, and artists and writers, dentists and pharmacists, social workers and engineers. And most recently, Howard has partnered with Google to bring more Black students into the tech industry. It prepared me for a career in public service, starting with my first-ever political race—for freshman class representative on what was then called the Liberal Arts Student Council.

So at this moment, when voices at the highest level of our government seem confused about the significance and even the constitutionality of supporting HBCUs, I say look over here at Howard University!

So now you are all official members of what I call the Role Model Club. And it's a pretty exclusive club. It includes my distinguished fellow commencement honorees. It includes members of the class of 1967, who today celebrate their fiftieth anniversary, and who marched and fought for justice when Jim Crow was still the law of the land. And it includes people like Charles Hamilton Hous-

ton and Thurgood Marshall, who were among my inspirations for going to law school.

History has proved that each generation of Howard graduates will forge the way forward for our country and our world. And now, it is your turn. And let's look at the world you are now entering.

———

But unlike telling the truth, speaking the truth means you must speak up and speak out. Even when you're not being asked, and even when it's uncomfortable or inconvenient.

———

You are graduating into a very different time than it was when you arrived a few short years ago. You are graduating into a time when we see a revival of the failed War on Drugs and a renewed reliance on mandatory minimum prison sentences. A time when young people who were brought to America as children fear a midnight knock on the door. A time when throwing millions of working people off their health insurance to give tax breaks to the top 1 percent is considered a victory to some. A time when we worry that a late-night tweet could start a war. A time when we no longer believe the words of some of our leaders, and where the very integrity of our justice system has been called into question.

Graduates, indeed we have a fight ahead. And it's not a fight between Democrats and

Republicans. It's not rich versus poor or urban versus rural. It's a fight to define what kind of country we are. It's a fight to determine what kind of country we will be. And it's a fight to determine whether we are willing to stand up for our deepest values. Because let's be clear— we are better than this. And you know what I'm talking about.

From the time you arrived on this campus, you participated in the fiftieth anniversary of the March on Washington, and you students have joined that fight for justice. You've protested, from the streets of Ferguson to the halls of the United States Congress. You have lived the words of James Baldwin: "There is never time in the future in which we will work out our salvation. The challenge is in the moment; the time is always now." Indeed, the time is always now. And because you are a Howard graduate, the bar is high. Which means you must be at the front of the line. You must be the first to raise your hand. You must lead.

The motto of this university is *Veritas et Utilitas*. "Truth and service." And I know sometimes we're afraid of falling short. It's not that we don't know what we should do. It's that the bar can sometimes feel too high. It takes so much time and effort to reach it, so much sweat and so many tears. And being human, we sometimes fall short. And that's okay. But because you went to Howard University, you have a responsibility to keep reaching for that bar. To keep serving.

So, class of 2017, proud members of the Role Model Club, in these unprecedented times, you must ask: How will I serve? How will I lead?

Well, I've got three pieces of advice on how to answer that question. Reject false choices. Speak truth. And don't think you need a big title to make a big difference. So let's talk about each of these.

First, to lead and thrive you must reject false choices. Howard taught me, as it has taught you, that you can do anything and you can do everything. At Howard, you can be a football player and a valedictorian. You can be a budding computer scientist and a poet. You can have a 4.0, intern on the Hill, and still find time to "darty" on the weekend. Back in the day, I'd go down to the National Mall to protest the United States' investment in apartheid South Africa. And I interned in the United States Senate. I chaired the Economics Society and was on the Howard debate team. And I pledged my dear sorority, Alpha Kappa Alpha. (In fact, several of my line sisters came here to be with me today.) So the notion of rejecting false choices that Howard taught us has carried me throughout my career—as the district attorney of San Francisco, as the attorney general of California, and now as a United States senator.

And in my career, the conventional wisdom was that people were either soft on crime or tough on crime. But I knew we should be smart on crime. I was told prosecutors don't need to focus on recidivism. People said, "That's not your job; just keep locking folks up." But as DA, I launched an initiative to help first-time offenders reenter society and not go back to

prison. I was told prosecutors shouldn't focus on the needs of children. But we created a Bureau of Children's Justice, that took on elementary school truancy.

So, graduates, I share all of this with you to make the point that there is no limit to what you can do when you detect and reject false choices. You can advocate for environmental justice, and you can be the CEO who commits to cutting your company's carbon footprint. You can march for workers on a picket line, and you can be their voice inside the Depart-

Above: About 250,000 demonstrators attended the March on Washington for Jobs and Freedom where Martin Luther King Jr. delivered his powerful "I Have a Dream" speech, August 28, 1963.

ment of Labor. You can call for greater diversity in the arts and entertainment, and you can be like Howard's own Taraji P. Henson on the screen, bringing to life those hidden figures. You can march for Black lives on the street, and you can ensure law enforcement accountability by serving as a prosecutor or on a police commission.

The reality is, on most matters, somebody is going to make the decision—so why not let it be you? Because if we're going to make progress anywhere, we need you everywhere. And, sometimes, to make change, you've got to change how change is made. So do not be constrained by tradition. Do not listen when they say it can't be done. And do not be burdened by what has been when you can create what should be. Like Baldwin said, the time is always now. So no false choices.

My second piece of advice is that you must speak truth. And let me be clear: Speaking the truth is different from telling the truth. Telling the truth means separating fact from fiction. The earth is round. The sky is blue. Howard University is the REAL H-U. But unlike telling the truth, speaking the truth means you must speak up and speak out. Even when you're not being asked, and even when it's uncomfortable or inconvenient.

Let me give you an example. Just a few years after I left Howard, I was working as a prosecutor during the crack epidemic in the 1990s. It was the height of gang violence in LA, and California had passed what were known as gang enhancement laws, which meant longer sentences if a person was affiliated with a gang. And because these laws were new, prosecutors were trying to figure out how to prove these cases in court.

So, one day I was in my office at the courthouse, and I heard my coworkers talking outside my door. They were talking about how they'd prove certain people were gang affiliated. So they mentioned the neighborhood where the arrest had occurred—the way the people were dressed, the kind of music they were listening to. And hearing this conversation, well, you know I had to poke my head outside my door. And I looked at them, and I said, "Hey, guys. You know that corner you were talking about? Well, I know people who live there. You

know the clothes you were talking about? I have family members who dress that way. And that music?"—and now I'm about to date myself—"Well, I have a tape of that music in my car." And in case you all are wondering, that tape was of Oakland's own Too Short. So they looked up, a little embarrassed. And needless to say, they realized they needed to think differently about who does what and where.

So Howard encourages us—expects us—to use our voice. And I promise you, as you leave this place, you will often find that you're the only one in the room who looks like you or who has had the same experience as you. And you're going to feel very alone. But wherever you are—whether you're in a courtroom, a boardroom, or a tech incubator, whether you're in Washington or Wichita—you must remember: You are never alone. Your entire Howard family, past and present—everyone here—will be in that room with you, cheering you on, as you speak up and speak out. The time is always now. Speak truth.

Here's my third piece of advice and final story. You don't need a big title to make a big difference.

So, after my second year of law school, I was a summer intern at the Alameda County DA's office, and there had been a big drug bust. And working on the case, I realized that among those arrested was an innocent bystander. But it was late on a Friday afternoon, and most people had gone home. Which meant the case wouldn't get called until Monday. Meaning this innocent bystander would have been held all weekend. And then I learned she had young children.

Now, no innocent person should spend a weekend in jail. And I knew what it would mean if she couldn't get home, including that she could even lose her children. So I sat right there in the courtroom and I waited. And waited. And waited. I told the clerk we had to call the case. I pleaded for the judge to come back. I wouldn't leave until the judge finally gave in. And when that happened, with the swipe of a pen, this woman got to go home to her children.

From the time you arrived on this campus, you participated in the fiftieth anniversary of the March on Washington, and you students have joined that fight for justice.

It would be years before I would run a major prosecutor's office, before I would create policies and write legislation that would be adopted at the state and national level. And I didn't realize it at the time, but that Friday afternoon in that courtroom in Oakland, California, that woman taught me that when you see something in front of you that's wrong, you can just go ahead and do what you know is right. And it will make a difference. Even if nobody but you and she knows. The time is always now. You don't need a big title to make a big difference.

So, graduates, as you begin this next phase of your life, I have one request of you. When you get your diploma later, take a good look at it. Remember what's on it? "Veritas" and "Utilitas." Truth and service. That is your duty—the duty of your degree. That is the charge of a Howard graduate.

So, whatever you plan to do next—whether you want to design the latest app or cure cancer or run a business, whether you're going to be a dentist, a lawyer, a teacher, or an accountant—let your guiding principle be truth and service. At a time when there are Americans—disproportionately Black and brown men—trapped in a broken system of mass incarceration, speak truth—and serve. At a time when men, women, and children have been detained at airports in our country simply because of the God they worship, speak truth—and serve. At a time when immigrants have been taken from their families in front of schools and outside courthouses, speak truth—and serve. And at a time of incredible scientific and technological advances as well, when we're dreaming of a mission to Mars, and unraveling the mysteries of the brain, and entrepreneurs in my home state of California are even starting to test flying cars, speak truth—and serve.

We need you. Our country needs you. The world needs you. Allyson, your HUSA president, said to me, "Boy, we can't wait until we're in charge." Well, guess what—I can't wait either. And neither can our world. So get out there. And your Howard family will be with you every step of the way. Congratulations! ■

Opposite: Kamala Harris campaigning to become San Francisco's next district attorney at the 24th Street BART station, October 2003; a pamphlet from the 2003 Harris campaign. **Above:** Kamala Harris's mother, Dr. Shyamala Gopalan Harris (center), holds a copy of the Bill of Rights while her daughter takes the oath of office to become San Francisco's district attorney, January 8, 2004.

San Francisco treasurer José Cisneros and District
Attorney Kamala Harris during a campaign event in 2005.

Previous pages: District Attorney Kamala Harris (right) smiles at Coni Binaley, campaign services coordinator, as she signs election papers launching her run for California attorney general, November 2008. **Above:** San Francisco district attorney Kamala Harris in October 2006. **Opposite:** District Attorney Harris at a 2010 civil rights rally in opposition to Proposition 8, a ballot proposition stating that "only marriage between a man and a woman is valid or recognized in California."

"*With [public service] comes a great amount of responsibility and power. But the power is supposed to be used in a responsible way . . . which requires a number of things— including some level of curiosity about how people are doing.*"

—**Kamala Harris**

San Francisco district attorney Kamala Harris at a 2010 press conference.

Opposite: Kamala Harris, candidate for California attorney general, answers questions from the media in downtown Los Angeles, September 27, 2010. **Above:** Lieutenant Governor Gavin Newsom and Attorney General Kamala Harris greet President Barack Obama upon his arrival to San Francisco in February 2011.

Above: Kamala Harris and Douglas Emhoff at the 24th Annual Beat the Odds Awards in December 2014. **Opposite:** Attorney Douglas Emhoff and California attorney general Kamala Harris at the 2014 LACMA Art + Film Gala in November 2014.

Jane Pauley: When you first got the friend who said, "There's a guy," maybe your friends were doing this to you all the time, "There's a guy, and he's a good one but don't Google him."

Kamala Harris: Yes.

Jane Pauley: You totally Googled him, didn't you?

Doug Emhoff: Ooh . . . this is a reveal.

Kamala Harris: I've never been asked that—I did!

—*CBS Sunday Morning* interview

Vice president elect Kamala Harris and her husband, Doug Emhoff, laughing during an interview on *CBS Sunday Morning*, January 2021.

> *We are here because we love our country and we firmly believe in the American ideal that our country should work for everyone.*
>
> **—Kamala Harris**

Above: California attorney general Kamala Harris speaking at the Democratic National Convention in Charlotte, North Carolina, 2012.
Opposite: With California representative Maxine Waters at the Democratic National Convention in Philadelphia, 2016.

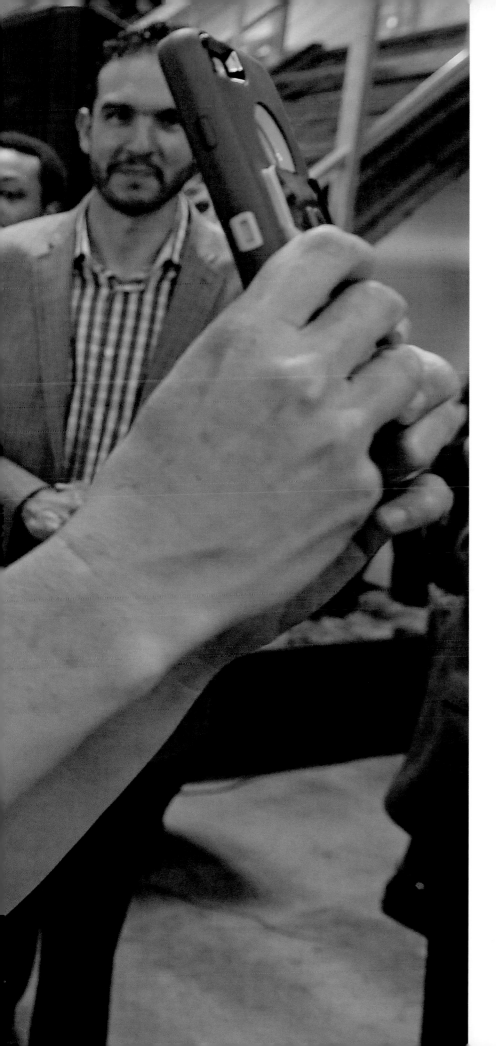

California attorney general Kamala Harris poses with (from left to right) Meiling Hunter and Alissa Harris after a news conference after California governor Jerry Brown endorsed Harris in the US Senate race, May 2016.

Influences

REPRESENTATION MATTERS

Representation matters in a working democracy. Our steps forward and backward in the United States can be measured in the history of African Americans in our legislative branches of government. During Reconstruction, the formerly enslaved made quick advancement in education, business, and politics. But then came the anti-Black backlash. Racial terrorism—including lynching—and suppression of the Black vote via poll taxes, literacy tests, and general harassment dammed the current of Black advancements. After the first generation of freedmen were pushed out of office, the United States would not have another African American senator for more than eight decades, until the 1960s with the election of Senator Edward Brooke. The African American groundbreakers in the Senate were as follows:

Hiram Rhodes Revels joined the Senate in 1870 as a Republican representing Mississippi. He had the rare privilege of being born to free people of color, an African American Baptist preacher and a mother with Scottish heritage, in North Carolina. He earned a reputation for being a powerful orator and a minister in the African Methodist Episcopal Zion Church.

Blanche Kelso Bruce escaped from slavery prior to Emancipation and served in the Senate representing Mississippi from 1875 to 1881.

Edward Brooke of Massachusetts, like his Black predecessors a Republican, served as a senator from 1967 to 1979. Born in Washington, DC, he, like his father and our vice president, attended Howard University.

Carol Moseley Braun was the first Black woman to serve in the Senate, from 1993 to 1999. She was a candidate for the Democratic nomination for president in 2004.

Barack Obama served as a senator from 2005 to 2008, at which point he successfully became the head of the Democratic ticket and the first African American president of the United States.

After the first generation of freedmen were pushed out of office, the United States would not have another African American senator for more than eight decades.

Opposite: Republican senator from Mississippi Blanche Kelso Bruce, ca. 1875.

Roland Burris, a Democrat from Illinois, was the first African American to win a statewide election in Illinois and became the Illinois attorney general. In 2009, he filled the Senate vacancy left by Barack Obama, but he did not run in the special election for the unexpired portion of the term. His service ended in November 2010.

Tim Scott, a Republican from South Carolina, was the first African American to represent a Southern state in the Senate since Reconstruction. He served one term as a US representative, was appointed US senator in 2013, and has been reelected since. His current term runs until 2022.

William "Mo" Cowan, a Democrat from Massachusetts and the former chief of staff for Massachusetts governor Deval Patrick, was appointed as US senator to fill the vacancy left by John Kerry, who resigned to join President Obama's cabinet. He served from February 1 to July 16, 2013.

Cory Booker, a Democrat from New Jersey, was mayor of Newark, New Jersey, from 2006 to 2013 and won his US Senate seat in 2013 in a special election to fill the vacancy left by the death of Frank Lautenberg. He's been reelected

twice since; his current term runs to 2027. He is the first African American US senator from New Jersey.

Kamala Harris served as US senator from California from 2017 until January 18, 2021, when she resigned to assume her new job as vice president of the United States. While in the Senate, she served on the Senate's Homeland Security and Government Affairs Committee, the Select Committee on Intelligence, the Committee on the Judiciary, and the Committee on the Budget.

Raphael G. Warnock is our most recent and eleventh Black senator and the first to serve in this role from Georgia. A senior pastor of Ebenezer Baptist Church in Atlanta, he is a graduate of Morehouse College, an HBCU, and Union Theological Seminary in New York. Kamala Harris's first task as vice president on inauguration day was to swear in Reverend Warnock and Jon Ossoff, who is the first Jewish senator to represent the state of Georgia. ■

Opposite: Democratic presidential candidate Bill Clinton and Illinois Democratic Senate candidate Carol Moseley Braun at a campaign stop in Illinois, July 29, 1992. **Above:** Senate candidate Reverend Raphael Warnock at a campaign rally in Stonecrest, Georgia, in December 2020.

Opposite: Official photo of US senator Kamala Harris. **Above:** Kamala Harris celebrates winning her Senate race in downtown Los Angeles on November 8, 2016. **Following pages:** From left to right: Senator Kamala Harris; her husband, Doug Emhoff; Vice President Joe Biden, Doug Emhoff's children, Ella and Cole; and Kamala Harris's sister, Maya, pose during Senator Kamala Harris's swearing-in ceremony on January 3, 2016.

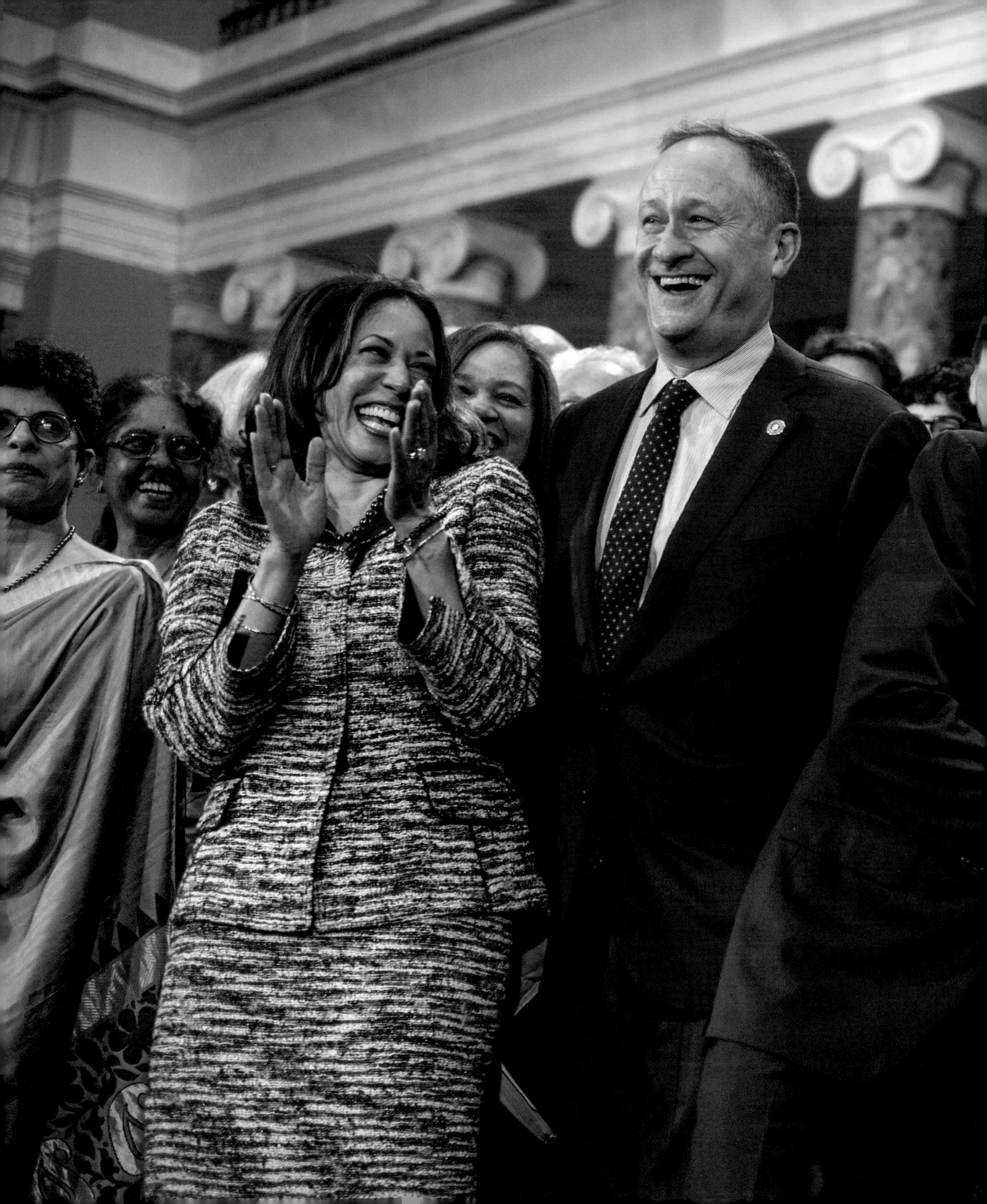

"There is nothing more powerful than a group of determined sisters marching alongside with their partners and their determined sons and brothers and fathers standing up for what we know is right."

—Kamala Harris

Kamala Harris addressing a crowd of protesters at the Women's March in Washington, DC, January 21, 2017.

Opposite: Senator Kamala Harris greets an officer at the Capitol as she arrives for work, February 3, 2020. **Above:** Listening to Christine Blasey Ford during a Senate Judiciary Committee hearing about Supreme Court nominee Brett Kavanaugh, September 27, 2018.

> **"** *I made the obvious connection between civil rights and public safety. I noticed when we file a criminal complaint, we don't write the name of the victim versus the name of the defendant. We write 'The People' versus the defendant.* **"**
>
> —**Kamala Harris**

Opposite: Senator Harris at the 2018 Worldwide Threat Assessment hearings of the Senate Intelligence Committee. **Above:** Senator Harris questioning Attorney General Jeff Sessions about his role in the firing of FBI director James Comey and the investigation into contacts between Trump campaign associates and Russia, June 13, 2017.

Speaking to reporters following a closed briefing on intelligence matters on Capitol Hill, December 4, 2018.

Above: (left to right) Senators Elizabeth Warren, Kamala Harris, and Sherrod Brown in the House Chamber during the State of the Union address, February 5, 2019. **Opposite:** Presidential candidate Senator Kamala Harris leaving the Capitol after voting on an amendment that would prohibit a US strike on Iran without congressional authorization, June 28, 2019.

> *She's always been a fighter, even from those early days. She always was sticking up for other people.*
>
> —**Wanda Kagan, high school classmate**

Senator Harris with reporters after walking out of an executive session of the Judicial Committee in protest over moving Supreme Court nominee Brett Kavanaugh's confirmation vote out of committee to the full senate, September 28, 2018.

We have to stand up and declare

the truth which is that our diversity

is our strength. And our unity is our

power. And that's part of what

Dr. King taught us . . . Let's recognize

the beauty of our community.

—Kamala Harris

Senator Harris celebrating Dr. Martin Luther King Jr.
and other activists at the 2018 Kingdom Day Parade
in Los Angeles, January 16, 2018.

97

"What I want young women and girls to know is: You are powerful and your voice matters. You're going to walk into many rooms in your life and career where you may be the only one who looks like you or who has had the experiences you've had. . . . So you use that voice and be strong."

—Kamala Harris

Senator Kamala Harris in the Senate Reception Room during President Trump's first impeachment trial, January 27, 2020.

January 20, 2021

Kamala Harris officially launched her presidential campaign on January 21, 2019, Martin Luther King Jr. Day. She was buoyed by a team of experienced campaign managers and a circle of prominent advisors that included three family members, all seasoned attorneys: her husband, Doug Emhoff; her brother-in-law, Tony West, who was a high-ranking official in the Justice Department in the Obama administration; and her sister, Maya Harris, who had been one of the three senior policy advisors to Hillary Clinton in 2016 and, for five years, the vice president for democracy, rights, and justice at the Ford Foundation. Maya would also serve as her campaign chair.

Twenty-nine men and women filed to run in the 2020 Democratic Party presidential primaries and caucuses, the largest field of major presidential candidates for any American political party since 1972, and the most diverse in its makeup. There were a half dozen women: Elizabeth Warren, Tulsi Gabbard, Amy Klobuchar, Marianne Williamson, Kirsten Gillibrand, and Kamala Harris. Three of the men were Black: Deval Patrick, Cory Booker, and Wayne Messam. Pete Buttigieg was openly gay, Andrew Yang was the son of Taiwanese immigrants, Julián Castro was

Previous pages: Vice President Kamala Harris gives President Joe Biden a pandemic-style greeting at the fifty-ninth presidential inauguration ceremony in Washington, DC, January 20, 2021. **Opposite:** Presidential hopeful Kamala Harris during a television interview after the second night of the first Democratic presidential debate in Miami, June 27, 2019.

of Mexican heritage, and Bernie Sanders and Michael Bloomberg were Jewish. Collectively, they are all born Americans and eligible, regardless of gender, race, religion, sexual orientation, or ethnicity, to become president of the United States.

Kamala was a front-runner at the outset but ended her campaign after eleven months, citing fundraising difficulties. But during that time, she had become memorable as a fearless contender. During one Democratic primary debate, she didn't miss an opportunity to call out Joe Biden for his opposition to school busing in the 1970s when he was a newly elected senator, reminding him that she was one of those young Black children to benefit from that program. In the days following that heated TV encounter, Biden clarified his position with her and with the media, saying his opposition was "mischaracterized." He supported the 1971 Supreme Court ruling that upheld the use of busing to achieve racial desegregation in schools but opposed it being ordered by the federal government instead of by desegregation programs initiated by local communities.

Biden was wise enough not to let that tense encounter prevent him from including Kamala on his list of VP candidates. Even before he became the presumptive Democratic presidential nominee, he announced he would choose a woman for his running mate. Many qualified women would be carefully considered. He announced his choice on April 8, 2020.

In its analysis of Biden's exhaustive review process, the *New York Times* reported that "in the end, Mr. Biden embraced Ms. Harris as a partner for reasons that were both pragmatic and personal. . . . No other candidate scored as highly with [his] selection committee on many of their core criteria for choosing a running mate, including her ability to help Mr. Biden win in November, her strength as a debater, her qualifications for governing and the racial diversity she would bring to the ticket. No other candidate seemed to match the political moment better." It also helped that Kamala was someone he knew long before they were adversaries in politics. She was a trusted friend of his late son, Beau Biden, when they were both attorneys general—she of California, he of Delaware—and worked together on housing policy issues.

Regardless of Kamala's experience, debating skills, and proven electability, Biden's choice of a Black woman was expected to create a

backlash, but it did not derail the ticket. As Robin Givhan commented in the *Washington Post*, "During the course of the campaign, the racists and misogynists reliably emerged to fling their insults and to try their best to diminish Harris. But even those dark words seemed to get lost in the immensity of the issues and emotions that defined this run for the presidency. Their vitriol just seemed to dissolve into the ether."

Another precedent that this first female vice president set is that there is for the first time a Second Gentleman. Kamala's husband, Doug Emhoff became "one of the unexpected breakout figures in the 2020 campaign, a headliner in the unconventional, pandemic-plagued race for the White House," as reporter Manuel Roig-Franzia put it. "He's the high-powered professional who has sidelined his career to support his wife's sky-high aspirations."

People who pay attention to such things anticipated that the double number 2020 portended an extraordinary year ahead for the United States,

Above: Presidential candidate Kamala Harris talking with farmer Matt Russell (center) and his husband, Patrick Standley, during her river-to-river bus tour across Iowa in August 2019.

and so it was: the election of the oldest man elected to be president of the United States; the first woman vice president; the COVID-19 pandemic; fires, floods, tornados, and other catastrophic environmental events and accidents; an expansion of the movement to end systemic racism, catalyzed by nationwide—and the most racially diverse ever—uprisings and Black Lives Matter; and an escalation of actions from an opposing force who fomented unrest through a movement called "MAGA," short for "make America great again," code for returning to the domination of

white men and a decline in support for democracy—factors that led to the January 6, 2021, invasion of the US Capitol for the first time since 1814.

A positive, hopeful sign came in November when the tide of Republican Party domination in Congress, which had begun to turn with the 2018 midterm elections, finally retreated with the decisive election of Democrats Joe Biden and Kamala Harris, and the unlikely hairbreadth victory in Georgia of two Democrats running for the US Senate—Raphael Warnock and Jon Ossoff. They would become the state of Georgia's first Black and first Jewish senators, respectively, and would give the new forty-sixth president the majority in both houses of Congress, which is now the most diverse in American history, according to a Pew Research report.

On January 20, 2021, Inauguration Day, Kamala Harris laid her hands on two Bibles—one belonged to Regina Shelton, the family friend who was a surrogate mother to her and her sister when their mother was away working, and the other belonged to her hero and inspiration, the late justice Thurgood Marshall. She was sworn in by another trailblazer, Supreme Court justice Sonia Sotomayor. When she took the oath of office to become vice president of the United States, she became the highest-ranking woman ever elected in American government. ◼

Above: Kamala Harris takes the stage at a campaign stop at Keene State College in New Hampshire, April 23, 2019. **Opposite:** President Biden's first weekly lunch with Vice President Harris, January 22, 2021.

We were raised in a community where we were taught to see a world beyond just ourselves, to be conscious and compassionate about the struggles of all people. We were raised to believe public service is a noble cause and the fight for justice is everyone's responsibility. In fact my mother used to say, 'Don't sit around and complain about things, do something.' . . . She was basically saying you gotta get up, and stand up, and don't give up the fight.

—Kamala Harris

Senator Kamala Harris announcing her candidacy for
president at Howard University, January 21, 2019.

Above: Senator Kamala Harris—holding her great-niece Amara—and Doug Emhoff wave to the crowd at Harris's first presidential campaign rally in her hometown of Oakland, California, January 27, 2019. **Opposite:** Presidential candidate Harris at the Asian and Latino Coalition event in the Iowa Statehouse where she spoke about immigration policy, college tuition, and gun control, February 23, 2019. Her sister and campaign chairwoman, Maya Harris, can be seen seated at left.

> "*Don't underestimate the Harris sisters. They're a force.*"
> —Shauna Marshall, Maya's law school mentor

Above: Kamala Harris with her sister and advisor, Maya Harris, preparing to speak during the Black Enterprise Women of Power Summit at the Mirage Hotel in Las Vegas, March 1, 2019. **Opposite:** At the Corinthian Baptist Church in Des Moines, August 11, 2019. **Following pages:** Twenty candidates appeared (a group of ten each night for two consecutive nights, June 26–27, 2019) during the first Democratic presidential debates in Miami. From left to right: former vice president Joe Biden, Vermont senator Bernie Sanders, and Senator Kamala Harris during one of the lighter moments.

"When I look at young girls and boys, and they look at me, they see themselves, and what they can be. That's the weight that I carry, and the joy of the weight."

—Kamala Harris

Previous pages: Democratic presidential candidate Harris showing off her moves at the Polk County Steak Fry on September 21, 2019, in Des Moines. **Left:** Presidential hopeful Kamala Harris with a drum line of fans at the "First in the West" event in the Bellagio Hotel ballroom in Las Vegas, November 17, 2019. Nevada was the first Western state to vote in the primaries.

Influences

ON HER SHOULDERS

*"You don't make progress
by standing on the
sidelines, whimpering
and complaining.
You make progress by
implementing ideas."*

—Shirley Chisholm

Vice President Kamala Harris's victory in 2021 marks the first time a woman has been elected to the executive branch of the United States government. The efforts to do so began more than 150 years ago when Elizabeth Cady Stanton, Lucretia Mott, and others convened the first women's rights convention of anti-slavery activists and suffragettes in Seneca Falls, New York, in 1848. Stanton was the first woman to run for a seat in Congress in 1866, as an independent. Many others have stood on the shoulders of these women in history and continue to pave a road to political power in the two-party system and outside of it. Today, one in four of our US congresspeople are women, the highest percentage in US history. Though the numbers still fall far short of women's share of our overall population, 144 of 539 seats is a 50 percent increase from a decade ago.

Among the trailblazing women to run for the highest office in the land are the following:

Victoria Claflin Woodhull ran for president before she or any other woman could legally vote, heading the Equal Rights Party ticket in 1872. She was a year younger than the constitutional requirement to be at least thirty-five years old. She announced a Black running mate, abolitionist Frederick Douglass. Oddly, though, he didn't join the campaign—because he never agreed to run.

Belva Ann Bennett Lockwood ran for president as the nominee of the Equal Rights Party in 1884 and 1888. Born in 1830, she drafted the law that admitted women to practice before the US Supreme Court, and she became the first woman lawyer to do so.

Margaret Chase Smith, a Republican, in 1964 became the first woman to have her name placed in nomination for president by a major party. Representing Maine, she served in the US House of Representatives (1940–49) and the US Senate (1949–73), the first woman to serve in both

Opposite: Presidential candidate Shirley Chisholm thanks delegates at the 1972 Democratic National Convention in Miami Beach, Florida.

houses of Congress. A former primary school teacher, she was reelected several times and served for four terms.

Shirley Anita Chisholm in 1968 was the first Black woman elected to the United States Congress, and in 1972 she was the first African American candidate as well as the first woman to run for the Democratic Party's presidential nomination. She was a daughter of immigrants from Barbados and an educator, and she began her political career as a volunteer in the Democratic political club in her Brooklyn birthplace. She served in the New York State Assembly from 1965 to 1968 and in the US House of Representatives from 1969 to 1983.

Patsy Takemoto Mink, a Japanese American lawyer, ran for president as an antiwar candidate in the Oregon Democratic primary in 1972. She was a member of the US House of Representatives from Hawaii from 1965 to 1977 and then returned to the US Congress in 1990, where she served until her death in 2002.

Ellen McCormack sought the Democratic presidential nomination as an antiabortion candidate in 1976 and ran as the nominee of the New York State Right to Life Party in 1980.

Geraldine Ferraro accepted Walter Mondale's and the Democratic Party's nomination for vice president in 1984, the first woman to receive such a nomination from a major party. "For a moment, for the Democratic Party and for an untold number of American women, anything seemed possible: a woman occupying the second-highest office in the land, a derailing of the Republican juggernaut," wrote Douglas Martin for the *New York Times*. His writing seems to have forecast a future that is now. Sonia Johnson also ran for president on the Citizens Party ticket in 1984; Lenora Fulani, an African American, ran as the New Alliance Party presidential candidate in 1988 and 1992; and Jill Stein was the Green Party presidential candidate in 2012 and 2016.

Elizabeth Hanford Dole sought the Republican nomination for president in 1999. She had been secretary of transportation (1983–87) and secretary of labor (1989–91) and served as a White House aide for both Johnson and Reagan. Alaska governor Sarah Palin was Senator John McCain's running mate in 2008, making her the first female vice presidential nominee for the Republican Party.

Carol Moseley Braun sought the Democratic nomination for president in 2004. A representative in the Illinois Legislature (1979–88), she was the first African American woman to serve in the Senate and did so for one term, from 1993 to 1999.

Cynthia McKinney, an African American former high school and university professor, was the Green Party nominee in 2008. She served six terms in the House, representing Georgia from 1992 to 2003 and then 2005 to 2007.

Michele Bachmann, a founder of the Tea Party Caucus, was a Republican candidate for president in 2012. She also served in the US Congress from 2007 to 2015 and was a Minnesota state senator from 2001 to 2007.

Carly Fiorina was the only woman who vied for the top of the Republican Party ticket in the 2016 election. As CEO of Hewlett-Packard, she was the first woman to head a Fortune 50 company.

Hillary Rodham Clinton is the only former First Lady to make a run for the presidency. She served in Barack Obama's cabinet as secretary of state from 2009 to 2013. Previously, she had been a US senator for New York from 2001 to 2009. She accepted the Democratic nomination for president in July 2016 and became the first woman to head a major party ticket. Her defeat by Donald J. Trump—even though she won the popular vote by more than 2.8 million votes—was arguably one of the most unexpected conclusions of a presidential race in modern times.

The *New York Times*'s Lisa Lerer and Glenn Thrush wrote in August 2020 that Kamala Harris is viewed "as a possible successor of sorts, a next-generation leader with the toughness to build on Mrs. Clinton's legacy." ■

Above: Vice presidential candidate Geraldine Ferraro with her husband, John Zaccaro, leaving their home in Queens, New York, in July 1984.

> *Your vote is your voice, and your voice is your power. Don't let anyone take away your power. Now is the time to stand up. Now is the time to speak out. And now is the time to vote.*
>
> **—Kamala Harris**

Kamala Harris addressing union members in Las Vegas, August 2019.

125

With fellow presidential candidate Senator Amy Klobuchar of Minnesota
at the West Des Moines Democrats Picnic, July 3, 2019.

Greeting supporters outside the New Hampshire Democratic Party State Convention, Manchester, New Hampshire, September 7, 2019.

"*I have no doubt that I picked the right person to join me as the next vice president of the United States of America, and that's Senator Kamala Harris. . . . Kamala knows how to govern. She knows how to make the hard calls. She is ready to do this job on day one.*"

—Joseph R. Biden Jr.

Opposite: With Joe Biden after endorsing him at a Detroit campaign rally on March 9, 2020. **Above:** Joe Biden admires his running mate during a virtual fundraising event at the Hotel Du Pont in Wilmington, Delaware, August 12, 2020.

> *I accept your nomination for vice president of the United States of America.*
>
> —**Kamala Harris**

Previous pages: Joe Biden and his wife, Jill Biden, wave to his vice presidential running mate, Kamala Harris, and her husband, Douglas Emhoff, after their first press conference together in Wilmington, Delaware, August 12, 2020. **Above:** A watch party at Tulsa, Oklahoma's Admiral Twin drive-in movie theater on the final night of the first-ever virtual Democratic National Convention, August 20, 2020. **Right:** Kamala Harris speaks before a socially distanced crowd during the Democratic National Convention in the midst of the COVID-19 pandemic, August 19, 2020.

A SEAT AT THE TABLE

Vice Presidential Nomination Acceptance Speech, Democratic National Convention,
Milwaukee, Wisconsin, August 19, 2020

Greetings, America. It is truly an honor to be speaking with you tonight. That I am here tonight is a testament to the dedication of generations before me. Women and men who believed so fiercely in the promise of equality, liberty, and justice for all. This week marks the one-hundredth anniversary of the passage of the Nineteenth Amendment, and we celebrate the women who fought for that right. Yet so many of the Black women who helped secure that victory were still prohibited from voting long after its ratification. But they were undeterred. Without fanfare or recognition, they organized and testified and rallied and marched and fought—not just for their vote, but for a seat at the table. These women and the generations that followed worked to make democracy and opportunity real in the lives of all of us who followed. They paved the way for the trailblazing leadership of Barack Obama and Hillary Clinton, and these women inspired us to pick up the torch and fight on. Women like Mary Church Terrell, Mary McLeod Bethune, Fannie Lou Hamer and Diane Nash, Constance

Left: Kamala Harris accepting her party's vice presidential nomination at the Democratic National Convention.

Baker Motley and the great Shirley Chisholm. We're not often taught their stories, but as Americans, we all stand on their shoulders.

And there's another woman whose name isn't known, whose story isn't shared. Another woman whose shoulders I stand on—and that's my mother, Shyamala Gopalan Harris. She came here from India at age nineteen to pursue her dream of curing cancer. At the University of California Berkeley, she met my father, Donald Harris, who had come from Jamaica to study economics. They fell in love in that most American way while marching together for justice in the civil rights movement of the 1960s. In the streets of Oakland and Berkeley, I got a stroller's-eye view of people getting into what the great John Lewis called "good trouble." When I was five, my parents split, and my mother raised us mostly on her own. Like so many mothers, she worked around the clock to make it work, packing lunches before we woke up and paying bills after we went to bed, helping us with homework at the kitchen table and shuttling us to church for choir practice. She made it look easy, though it never was. My mother instilled in my sister Maya and me the values that would chart the course of our lives. She raised us to be proud, strong Black women, and she raised us to know and be proud of our Indian heritage. She taught us to put family first—the family you're born into and the family you choose.

Family is my husband, Doug, who I met on a blind date set up by my best friend. Family is our beautiful children, Cole and Ella, who call me Mamala. Family is my sister; family is my best friend, my nieces, and my godchildren. Family is my uncles, my aunts, and my *chitthis*. Family is Mrs. Shelton, my second mother, who lived two doors down and helped raise me. Family is my beloved Alpha Kappa Alpha, our Divine Nine and my HBCU brothers and sisters. Family is the friends I turned to when my mother—the most important person in my life—passed away from cancer. And even as she taught us to keep our family at the center of our world, she also pushed us to see a world beyond ourselves. She taught us to be conscious and compassionate about the struggles of all people, to believe public service is a noble cause and the fight for justice is a shared responsibility. That led me to become a lawyer, a district attorney, attorney general, and a United States senator. And at every step of the way I've been guided by the words I spoke from the first time I stood in a courtroom: "Kamala Harris for the people." I have fought for children and survivors of sexual assault. I fought against transnational criminal organizations. I took on the biggest banks and helped take down one of the biggest for-profit colleges. I know a predator when I see one.

My mother taught me that service to others gives life purpose and meaning. And oh, how I wish she were here tonight, but I know she's looking down on me from above. I keep thinking about that twenty-five-year-old Indian woman—all of five feet tall—who gave birth to me at Kaiser Hospital in Oakland, California. On that day, she probably could have never imagined that I would be standing before you now and speaking these words: I accept your nomination for vice president of the United States of America. I do so committed to the values she taught me, to the word that teaches me to walk by faith and not by sight, and to a vision passed on through generations of Americans, one that Joe Biden shares. A vision of our nation as a beloved community where all are welcome no matter what we look like, no matter where we come from or who we love. A country where we may not agree on every detail, but we are united by the fundamental belief that every human being is of infinite worth, deserving of compassion, dignity, and respect. A country where we look out for one another, where we rise and fall as one, where we face our challenges and celebrate our triumphs together.

Today, that country feels distant. Donald Trump's failure of leadership has cost lives and livelihoods. If you're a parent struggling with your child's remote learning or you're a teacher struggling on the other side of that screen, you know what we're doing right now is not working. And we are a nation that is grieving. Grieving the loss of life, the loss of jobs, the loss of opportunities, the loss of normalcy, and, yes, the loss of certainty. And while this virus touches us all, we've got to be honest: It is not an equal opportunity offender. Black, Latino, and Indigenous people are suffering and dying disproportionately, and this is not a coincidence; it is the effect of structural racism, of inequities in education and technology, health care and housing, job security and transportation, the injustice in reproductive and maternal health care, and the excessive use of force by police, and in our broader criminal justice system. This virus, it has no eyes, and yet it knows exactly how we see each other and how we treat each other. And let's be clear: There is no vaccine for racism. We've got to do the work for George Floyd, for Breonna Taylor, for the lives of too many others to name, for our children, and for all of us. We've got to do the work to fulfill that promise of equal justice under law, because here's the thing: None of us are free until all of us are free.

So, we're at an inflection point. The constant chaos leaves us adrift; the incompetence makes us feel afraid; the callousness makes us feel alone. It's a lot, and here's the thing: We can do better and deserve so much more. We must elect a president who will bring something different, something better, and do the important work. A president who will bring all of us together—Black, white, Latino, Asian, Indigenous—to achieve the future we collectively want. We must elect Joe Biden. And I will tell you, I knew Joe as vice president, I knew Joe on the campaign trail, and I first got to know

Joe as the father of my friend. So, Joe's son Beau and I served as attorneys general of our states, Delaware and California. During the Great Recession, he and I spoke on the phone nearly every day, working together to win back billions of dollars for homeowners from the big banks that foreclosed on people's homes. And Beau and I, we would talk about his family, how as a single father Joe would spend four hours every day riding the train back and forth from Wilmington to Washington. Beau and Hunter got to have breakfast every morning with their dad, they went to sleep every night with the sound of his voice reading bedtime stories. And while they endured an unspeakable loss, those two little boys always knew that they were deeply, unconditionally loved. And what also moved me about Joe is the work that he did as he was going back and forth. This is the leader who wrote the Violence Against Women Act and enacted the Assault Weapons Ban. Who, as vice president, implemented the Recovery Act, which brought our country back from the Great Recession. He championed the Affordable Care Act—protecting millions of Americans with pre-existing conditions. Who spent decades promoting American values and interests around the world. Joe—he believes we stand with our allies and stand up to our adversaries. Right now, we have a president who turns our tragedies into political weapons. Joe will be a president who turns our challenges into purpose. Joe will bring us together to build an economy that doesn't leave anyone behind, where a good-paying job is the floor, not the ceiling. Joe will bring us together to end this pandemic and make sure that we are prepared for the next one. Joe will bring us together to squarely face and dismantle racial injustice, furthering the work of generations. Joe and I believe that we can build that beloved community, one that is strong and decent, just and kind, one in which we can all see ourselves. That's the vision that our parents and grandparents fought for, the vision that made my own life possible, the vision that makes the American promise—for all its complexities and imperfections—a promise worth fighting for.

So, make no mistake, the road ahead is not easy. We may stumble, we may fall short, but I pledge to you that we will act boldly and deal with our challenges honestly. We will speak truths, and we will act with the same faith in you that we ask you to place in us. We believe that our country—all of us—will stand together for a better future, and we already are. We see it in the doctors, the nurses, the home health care workers, and frontline workers who are risking their lives to save people they've never met. We see it in the teachers and truck drivers, the factory workers and farmers, the postal workers and poll workers, all putting their own safety on the line to help us get through this pandemic. And we see it in so many of you who are working—not just to get us through our current crisis but to somewhere better. There's something happening all across our country. It's not about Joe or me; it's about you, and it's about us. People of all ages and colors and creeds who are, yes, tak-

ing to the streets and also persuading our family members, rallying our friends, organizing our neighbors, and getting out the vote. And we have shown that when we vote, we expand access to health care and expand access to the ballot box and ensure that more working families can make a decent living. And I'm so inspired by a new generation—you, you are pushing us to realize the ideals of our nation, pushing us to live the values we share: decency and fairness, justice and love. You are patriots who remind us that to love our country is to fight for the ideals of our country.

In this election, we have a chance to change the course of history. We're all in this fight—you, me, and Joe—together. What an awesome responsibility, what an awesome privilege. So, let's fight with conviction, let's fight with hope, let's fight with confidence in ourselves and a commitment to each other, to the America we know is possible, the America we love. And years from now this moment will have passed, and our children and our grandchildren will look in our eyes, and they're going to ask us, "Where were you when the stakes were so high?" They will ask us, "What was it like?" And we will tell them. We will tell them not just how we felt; we will tell them what we did. Thank you, God bless you, and God bless the United States of America. ■

Opposite: Presidential candidate Joe Biden enjoys the fireworks with his running mate, Kamala Harris, and his wife, Jill Biden, as the 2020 Democratic National Convention comes to a close, August 20, 2020.

And protecting our democracy takes struggle. It takes sacrifice.

But there is joy in it. And there is progress. Because we, the

people, have the power to build a better future.

—Kamala Harris

Kamala Harris with virtual viewers on the last night of the Democratic National Convention at the Chase Center in Wilmington, Delaware, August 20, 2020.

> *Mr. Vice President, I'm speaking. I'm speaking . . . If you don't mind letting me finish, then we can have a conversation.*
>
> **—Kamala Harris**

Left: Kamala Harris sparring with Mike Pence during the vice presidential debate held in Kingsbury Hall at the University of Utah in Salt Lake City on October 7, 2020. **Following pages:** Senator Kamala Harris during the vice presidential debate with Vice President Mike Pence, October 7, 2020.

And do you know that of the fifty people who President Trump appointed to the Court of Appeals for lifetime appointments, not one is Black? This is what they've been doing. You want to talk about packing a court? Let's have that discussion.

—Kamala Harris

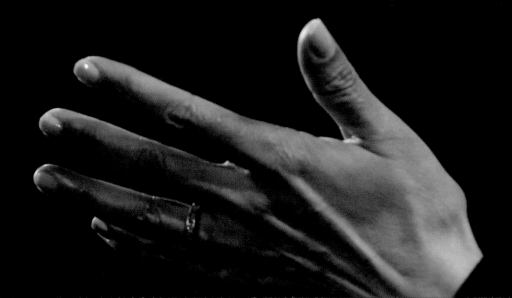

Influences

CHUCKS & PEARLS

What they wear. The music they listen to. The food they eat and cook. The way they dance—if they dance. How they spend their time when they are and are not attending to the business of the nation. All of these minutiae about high-profile politicians fascinate supporters, critics, and media in equal measure—especially when that politician is Vice President Kamala Harris.

On the campaign trail, for the most part, she's worn the uniform of all powerful women: well-fitted pantsuits, silk blouses with feminine necklines, pearls, heels, and hair that's coifed but moves—bouncing and behaving, as Black women say among ourselves. She dressed to impress but not to detour the conversation away from the critical issues of our time. Her other look—exiting a plane, visiting voters on the campaign trail, taking long walks with her husband—is either athletic wear that is neither dowdy nor sexy, or, most often, classic jeans and Converse sneakers, affectionately known as Chuck Taylors, with a strand of pearls.

When the topic of food comes up, as the *Times of India* reports, "Whether it's doing an innocent cooking tutorial showing how to rustle up that perfect tuna melt or making masala dosa with actor and writer Mindy Kaling . . . one cannot separate Kamala from her food."

She knows how to get down to the business of government, make a Sunday meal with her family a ritual, or move in rhythm to music. She, as we say, gets real. In her father's home country, the number one newspaper, the *Gleaner*, quotes her fans there saying they can tell she's a "real" Jamaican by the way she moves to music. One mark of the pride she invokes is the lyric she inspired Jamaican reggae/dancehall performer Nadine Sutherland to write: "Action, not a bag a mouth. She clean when she step inna the White House." "Clean is a term used initially in the street culture of Jamaica that [came into wider use] in the general Jamaican populace," Sutherland says. "It's a complimentary exchange amongst women, that in this case means Kamala showed up fresh, beautiful, nice, and fabulous in the White House."

All over the US and beyond, women and girls celebrated the inauguration by posting photographs of themselves looking like Kamala, wearing Chucks, pearls, and proud smiles. ■

Opposite: Vice presidential candidate Kamala Harris at the Social Status boutique in Charlotte, North Carolina, taking a look at the special Converse Chuck Taylor All-Star sneakers designed by Nina Chanel Abney. The shoes, inspired by the senator, were donated to students at local HBCU Johnson C. Smith University.

Opposite: San Francisco district attorney Kamala Harris shows off her signature pearls along with her pearly whites as she greets President Obama in San Francisco, October 2010. **Above:** Attorney General Harris on the road during her Fearless for the People tour/run for the Senate in November 2016.

Above: It's all in the tiny details. Allison Hoffman's crochet Kamala doll in pantsuit and Chucks. Patterns available from craftyiscool.com. **Opposite:** Joseph Biden and Kamala Harris action figures from FCTRY.com, sculpted by Seattle-based artist and activist Mike Leavitt. Like Mike's fine-art pieces, the figures are one part product and one part social commentary, exploring who we idolize in contemporary culture and how we do it.

"*The design symbolizes two powerful women (of color) in history. . . . Ruby walked into a white-dominated school, and that took courage and made history. Kamala is walking into a white-dominated White House. . . . They have both changed the game of representation. Nothing is finished. But both will be seen as firsts.*"

—Bria Goeller

Above: *The Little Girl Was Me* by Bria Goeller, created for Good Trouble (WTF America) in 2020, is an illustration inspired by Norman Rockwell's iconic 1964 painting *The Problem We All Live With*. The shadow in Goeller's illustration represents the six-year-old student Ruby Bridges, seen in Rockwell's painting on her way to school during desegregation. **Opposite:** A piece of street art from artist SacSix's #SidewalksAndIcons series pasted up on Rivington Street on the Lower East Side of Manhattan in 2020.

Biden-Harris supporters at a drive-in rally
in Philadelphia on November 1, 2020.

TEXT UNITED TO 30330

BATTLE for the

"My mother would look at me and she'd say, 'Kamala, you may be the first to do many things, but make sure you are not the last.'"

—Kamala Harris

Previous pages: As the race comes to a close, VP nominee Kamala Harris speaks during a drive-in campaign in Philadelphia on November 2, 2020. **Above:** Kamala Harris and husband, Douglas Emhoff, on stage in Philadelphia as Scranton-born Joe Biden speaks in Pittsburgh at a simultaneous drive-in election eve rally on November 2, 2020. **Opposite:** Onstage in Wilmington, Delaware, celebrating the Biden-Harris victory, November 7, 2020.

Speech

THE VICTORY SPEECH

Wilmington, Delaware, November 7, 2020

Good evening.

Congressman John Lewis, before his passing, wrote, "Democracy is not a state. It is an act." And what he meant was that America's democracy is not guaranteed. It is only as strong as our willingness to fight for it, to guard it and never take it for granted.

And protecting our democracy takes struggle. It takes sacrifice. There is joy in it, and there is progress. Because We the People have the power to build a better future.

And when our very democracy was on the ballot in this election, with the very soul of America at stake, and the world watching, you ushered in a new day for America.

To our campaign staff and volunteers, this extraordinary team—thank you for bringing more people than ever before into the democratic process and for making this victory possible.

To the poll workers and election officials across our country who have worked tirelessly to make sure every vote is counted—our nation owes you a debt of gratitude, as you have protected the integrity of our democracy.

And to the American people who make up our beautiful country—thank you for turning out in record numbers to make your voices heard. I know times have been challenging, especially the last several months. The grief, sorrow, and pain. The worries and the struggles. But we've also witnessed your courage, your resilience, and the generosity of your spirit.

For four years, you marched and organized for equality and justice, for our lives, and for our planet. And then, you voted. You delivered a clear message. You chose hope, unity, decency, science, and, yes, truth. You chose Joe Biden as the next president of the United States of America.

Joe is a healer. A uniter. A tested and steady hand. A person whose own experience of loss gives him a sense of purpose that will help us, as a nation, reclaim our own sense of purpose. And a man with a big heart who loves with abandon. It's his love for Jill, who will be an incredible First Lady. It's his love for Hunter, Ashley, his grandchildren, and the entire Biden family. And while I first knew Joe as vice president, I really got to know him as the father who loved Beau, my dear friend, who we remember here today.

To my husband, Doug; our children, Cole and Ella; my sister, Maya; and our whole family—I love you all more than I can express. We are so grateful to Joe and Jill for welcoming our family into theirs on this incredible journey. And to the woman most responsible for my presence here today—my mother, Shyamala Gopalan Harris, who is always in our hearts. When she came here from India at the age of nineteen, maybe she didn't quite imagine this moment. But she believed so deeply in an America where a moment like this is possible.

So, I'm thinking about her and about the generations of women—Black women, Asian, white, Latina, and Native American women throughout our nation's history who have paved the way for this moment tonight. Women who fought and sacrificed so much for equality, liberty, and justice for all, including the Black women, who are too often overlooked, but so often prove that they are the backbone of our democracy. All the women who worked to secure and protect the right to vote for over a century: one hundred years ago with the Nineteenth Amendment, fifty-five years ago with the Voting Rights Act, and now, in 2020, with a new generation of women in our country who cast their ballots and continued the fight for their fundamental right to vote and be heard. Tonight, I reflect on their struggle, their determination, and the strength of their vision—to see what can be unburdened by what has been. I stand on their shoulders.

And what a testament it is to Joe's character that he had the audacity to break one of the most substantial barriers that exists in our country and select a woman as his vice president.

But while I may be the first woman in this office, I will not be the last. Because every little girl watching tonight sees that this is a country of possibilities.

And to the children of our country, regardless of your gender, our country has sent you a clear message: Dream with ambition, lead with conviction, and see yourself in a way that others might not see you, simply because they've never seen it before. And we will applaud you every step of the way.

To the American people: No matter who you voted for, I will strive to be the vice president that Joe was to President Obama—loyal, honest, and prepared, waking up every day thinking of you and your families. Because now is when the real work begins. The hard work. The necessary work. The good work. The essential work to save lives and beat this pandemic. To rebuild our economy so it works for working people. To root out systemic racism in our justice system and society. To combat the climate crisis. To unite our country and heal the soul of our nation.

The road ahead will not be easy. But America is ready. And so are Joe and I. We have elected a president who represents the best in us. A leader the world will respect and our children can look up to. A commander in chief who will respect our troops and keep our country safe. And a president for all Americans.

It is now my great honor to introduce the president-elect of the United States of America, Joe Biden. ■

Previous pages: One of the many spontaneous celebrations—this one in New York's Times Square—that sprung up on Saturday, November 7, 2020, moments after Joe Biden was finally projected to have enough electoral votes to win the presidency. **These pages:** Jennifer Lopez sings "This Land Is Your Land" and "America the Beautiful" at the fifty-ninth presidential inauguration ceremony in Washington, January 20, 2021.

"When she takes the oath of office, little girls and boys across the world will know that anything and everything is possible. And in the end, that is America.

—Senator Amy Klobuchar

Opposite: Los Angeles artist Glen Hanson's illustration *Inauguration Ladies*—an homage to the powerful women at the January 20, 2021, event—went viral on Instagram. **Above:** Amanda Gorman, poet, activist, and former National Youth Poet Laureate, steps to the podium before dazzling the crowd with her inaugural poem, "The Hill We Climb."

> " *I, Kamala Devi Harris, do solemnly swear that I will support and defend the Constitution of the United States against all enemies, foreign and domestic; that I will bear true faith and allegiance to the same; that I take this obligation freely, without any mental reservation or purpose of evasion; that I will well and faithfully discharge the duties of the office upon which I am about to enter. So help me God.* "

Kamala Harris is sworn in as vice president by Supreme Court Justice Sonia Sotomayor as her husband, Doug Emhoff, holds the two Bibles.

> *Emhoff chose to wear a gray suit by Ralph Lauren, which he paired with a black mask and gloves, a dark tie, and a small flag pin on the lapel of his overcoat. . . . His subdued aesthetic allowed for his wife to shine, in her striking purple coat and dress designed by Christopher John Rogers.*

—Caroline Hallemann (*Town & Country* magazine)

Above: Newly sworn-in vice president Kamala Harris and her husband, Second Gentleman Doug Emhoff, walk down Pennsylvania Avenue toward the White House during the inaugural parade, January 20, 2021. **Opposite:** Vice President Kamala Harris and her husband, Doug Emhoff, climb the Navy Steps of the Eisenhower Executive Office Building at the White House to visit the vice president's ceremonial office for the first time, January 20, 2021.

After being sworn in as president, Joseph R. Biden Jr., and Vice President Kamala Harris visit the Tomb of the Unknown Soldier at Arlington National Cemetery and pause for a moment of silence during a wreath-laying ceremony. Also attending were former First Ladies Michelle Obama and Laura Bush, former presidents Barack Obama and Bill Clinton, and former First Lady and secretary of state Hillary Clinton. The ceremony was hosted by US Army major general Omar Jones IV (standing next to Harris).

> *Even in dark times—We not only dream. We do.*
> *We not only see what has been; we see what can be.*
> *We shoot for the moon, and then we plant our flag*
> *on it. We are bold, fearless, and ambitious. We are*
> *undaunted in our belief that we shall overcome, that*
> *we will rise up. This is American aspiration.*

—Kamala Harris

Above and **Opposite:** Vice President Kamala Harris and Second Gentleman Doug Emhoff listening to Katy Perry at the Lincoln Memorial during the Celebrate America inaugural special, January 20, 2021.

Opposite: President Joe Biden and Vice President Kamala Harris in the Oval Office after the president signed executive orders strengthening Americans' access to quality, affordable health care, January 26, 2021.
Above: Vice President Harris with Second Gentleman Doug Emhoff in her West Wing Office at the White House.

Above: The vice president reviewing notes with staff members in her office at the White House, February 2021. **Left:** Vice President Kamala Harris on the Senate floor casts the tie-breaking vote—her first—paving the way for fast-track passage of President Biden's $1.9 trillion coronavirus relief plan without support from Republicans, February 5, 2021. **Opposite:** VP Kamala Harris with UNLV medical students Lauren Hollifield and Mailani Thompson as the COVID-19 vaccine rollout ramps up in March 2021.

Opposite: The vice president preparing to record a video address in the State Dining Room of the White House, March 9, 2021. **Above**: Vice President Kamala Harris visiting Fibre Space, a small business in Old Town Alexandria, Virginia, to discuss the White House's American Rescue Plan, which provides pandemic relief to struggling families, March 3, 2021.

"*For many months, we have grieved by ourselves. Tonight, we grieve and begin healing together. Though we may be physically separated, we, the American people, are united in spirit, and my abiding hope, my abiding prayer, is that we emerge from this ordeal with a new wisdom, to cherish simple moments, to imagine new possibilities, and to open our hearts just a little bit more to one another.*"

—**Kamala Harris**

Doug Emhoff, Kamala Harris, Jill Biden, and Joe Biden share a quiet moment at the reflecting pool of the Lincoln Memorial during a service honoring the nearly 400,000 American victims of the COVID-19 pandemic on the eve of the inauguration, January 19, 2021.

ACKNOWLEDGMENTS

Thank you to Esther Margolis of Newmarket Publishing Management for inviting me to join the team, including designer Timothy Shaner and photo editor Christopher Measom of Night & Day Design, to create this book. Doing the research and writing the narrative was a perfect way for me to process some of the most dramatic collective events of our time on planet Earth and left me feeling more optimistic than ever about the American story, past, present, and future.

Thank you to our editor, Barbara Berger, and everyone at Sterling Publishing who did all the jobs that book professionals do. Though you may not be widely regarded as such, I believe you are essential workers not only to an industry, but to our culture. May you continue and grow.

Books have been central to my life's work, and I've been privileged to work on scores of them that brought readers and me joy. This one is special and will remain so because it documents an accomplishment that promises to change the course of my life in particular as a Black woman and our nation for good forever. And for that, I thank my fellow Americans who voted in the 2020 presidential election and those activists and leaders who protected their voting rights.

—MALAIKA ADERO, April 2021

NOTES

INTRODUCTION: I'M SPEAKING

Page 2: **"While I may be the first"**: "Read the Transcript of Kamala Harris's Victory Speech in Wilmington, Del.," *Washington Post*, November 7, 2020. **"The most insignificant Office"**: "John Adams to Abigail Adams, 19 December 1793," Founders Online, National Archives. **"I don't want to work"**: "Thomas R. Marshall, 28th Vice President (1913–1921)," United States Senate website. **"the last voice in the room . . . hard questions"**: Ben Gittleson, "Kamala Harris Slowly Starts to Carve Out Role beyond 'Making Sure Joe Biden Is a Success,'" ABCNews.com, February 17, 2021.

Page 4: **"I, Kamala Devi Harris"**: Elissa Nadworny, "Kamala Harris Sworn in as Vice President," NPR, January 20, 2021.

Page 5: **"We have a lot"**: Kamala Harris (@KamalaHarris), Twitter, December 11, 2020.

PART ONE: AN AMERICAN GIRL

Page 10: **"a crucible of radical politics"**: Ellen Barry, "How Kamala Harris's Immigrant Parents Found a Home, and Each Other, in a Black Study Group," *New York Times*, September 12, 2020. **"Going against traditions"**: "Attorney General Inaugural Address—January 3, 2011," Archives of Women's Political Communication, Iowa State University.

Page 11: **"ready for company"**: Kamala Harris, *The Truths We Hold: An American Journey* (New York: Penguin, 2019), 75. **"would run the gamut"**: Donna Owens, "VP Kamala Harris Inspires Women and Girls to Dream Big," *Essence*, January 20, 2021. **"My parents and their friends"**: Harris, *The Truths We Hold*, 10. **"a sea of legs"**: Harris, *The Truths We Hold*, 8. **"What do you want?"**: Harris, *The Truths We Hold*, 8.

Page 12: **"We would see [my father]"**: Harris, *The Truths We Hold*, 6. **"Everyone in the neighborhood"**: Harris, *The Truths We Hold*, 17. **"a richness of conscience"**: Kamala Harris, "UCLA Law School Commencement Address—May 13, 2009," Archives of Women's Political Communication, Iowa State University. **"I only learned later"**: Harris, *The Truths We Hold*, 11. **"How wonderful it was"**: Harris, *The Truths We Hold*, 11. **"an unassuming beige building"**: Harris, *The Truths We Hold*, 16.

Page 14: **"My mother was the strongest person"**: Harris, *The Truths We Hold*, 145.

Page 15: **"Her childhood friends recalled"**: Dan Bilefsky, "Kamala Harris's 'Canadian Dream,'" *New York Times*, October 9, 2020. **"During high school"**: Harris, *The Truths We Hold*, 20. **"When I was a kid"**: Harris, *The Truths We Hold*, 254.

Page 16: **"one of the highest callings"**: "The Truths We Hold" [interview with Kamala Harris], CSPAN, January 9, 2019. **"had cut a deal"**: "Attorney General Inaugural Address—January 3, 2011." **"in a household"**: Harris, *The Truths We Hold*, 7. **"skilled community organizer"**: Harris, *The Truths We Hold*, 7. **"had been part of the movement"**: Harris, *The Truths We Hold*, 7.

Page 18: "Harris comes from": Janet Silvera, "Kamala Harris Ignites Pride in Brown's Town," the *Gleaner*, August 16, 2020.

Page 21: "For a long time": Meena Harris (@meena), Instagram, July 28, 2019.

Page 23: "There was a richness": Kamala Harris, "UCLA Law School Commencement Address—May 13, 2009," Archives of Women's Political Communication, Iowa State University.

Page 24: "total exposition": "Interview with Mary Ann Pollar at Rainbow Sign," KRON, April 26, 1975. **"a hub for black art":** Anne Brice, "Inside Rainbow Sign, a Vibrant Hub for Black Cultural Arts," *Berkeley News*, September 19, 2017. **"a Jewish organization":** "The Rainbow Sign," The Berkeley Revolution: A Digital Archive of the East Bay's Transformation in the Late 1960s and 1970s [website hosted by the University of California at Berkeley].

PART TWO: A PURSUIT OF JUSTICE

Page 35: "Though the seed was planted": Harris, *The Truths We Hold*, 20. **"a wonderful place . . . alma mater":** Harris, *The Truths We Hold*, 21. **Page 36: "I'll always remember":** Harris, *The Truths We Hold*, 22. **"Howard was a place":** Robin Givhan, "Kamala Harris Made History with Quiet, Exquisite Power," *Washington Post*, November 7, 2020. **"I dove":** Harris, *The Truths We Hold*, 23.

Page 38: "'I wouldn't have been able'": Harris, *The Truths We Hold*, 214. **"I loved going to the Capitol":** Harris, *The Truths We Hold*, 24. **"a legacy":** Kamala Harris, "Commencement Address at Howard University," May 13, 2017. **"I pretty much":** Kamala Harris, "San Francisco State University Commencement Address," May 26, 2007. **"made the obvious connection":** Harris, "UCLA Law School Commencement Address."

Page 39: "I was going to do the [prosecutor] job": Harris, *The Truths We Hold*, 26.

Page 40: "I wasn't running": Harris, *The Truths We Hold*, 40. **"My mother often took charge":** Harris, *The Truths We Hold*, 39. **"Our campaign attracted":** Harris, *The Truths We Hold*, 41. **"'get-it-done' progressive":** Gene Demby, "Let's Talk about Kamala Harris," NPR, October 14, 2020. **"There was no such thing":** Demby, "Let's Talk about Kamala Harris."

Page 41: "A woman running": Harris, *The Truths We Hold*, 83.

Page 42: "Mommy, these guys": Harris, *The Truths We Hold*, 210. **"When you break":** Harris, *The Truths We Hold*, 279.

Page 43: "Family means everything": Kamala Harris, Instagram, September 6, 2020. **"This is a moment":** *Good Morning America*, January 21, 2019.

Page 44: "The campus was a place": Harris, *The Truths We Hold*, 22.

Page 49: "Family is my beloved": Christina Wilkie, "Here's What Kamala Harris Said at the Democratic National Convention,"cnbc.com, August 19, 2020.

Page 64: "With [public service]": "The Truths We Hold" [interview with Kamala Harris], CSPAN, January 9, 2019.

Page 71: "Jane Pauley: When you first": "Kamala Harris and Douglas Emhoff on breaking new ground," *CBS Sunday Morning*, interview with Jane Pauley, January 17, 2021.

Page 72: "We are here because": "California Attorney General Kamala Harris Addresses 2012 Democratic National Convention" [video], CSPAN, September 5, 2012.

Page 85: "There is nothing more powerful": "Women Lawmakers Address Women's March on Washington" [video], CSPAN, January 21, 2017.

Page 89: "I made the obvious connection": Harris, "UCLA Law School Commencement Address," 2009.

Page 94: "She's always been a fighter": Casey Tolan, "Why Some of Kamala Harris' Biggest Fans Are in Canada," *Mercury News*, May 7, 2019.

Page 97: "We have to stand up": "US Senator Kamala Harris at the Kingdom Day Parade Breakfast 2018" [video], richgirlnetwork.tv, January 19, 2018.

Page 98: "What I want young women": Kayla Webley Adler, "One of These Women Could Be Our Next President," *Marie Claire*, February 21, 2019.

PART THREE: SHE LEADS

Page 104: "in the end": Alexander Burns, Jonathan Martin, and Katie Glueck, "How Biden Chose Harris: A Search That Forged New Stars, Friends, and Rivalries," *New York Times*, August 13, 2020.

Page 105: "During the course": Givhan, "Kamala Harris Made History." **"one of the unexpected":** Manuel Roig-Franzia, "Doug Emhoff Paused His Career for His Wife Kamala Harris's Aspirations—and Became the Campaign's 'Secret Weapon,'" *Washington Post*, October 28, 2020.

Page 108: "We were raised": "Senator Kamala Harris Presidential Campaign Launch in Oakland, CA" [video], CSPAN, January 27, 2019.

Page 112: "Don't underestimate": Cameron Joseph, "Sister Action: Kamala and Maya Harris Tag-Team the Fight for the White House," talkingpointsmemo.com, April 12, 2019.

Page 119: "When I look at": Kamala Harris, Instagram, September 28, 2020.

Page 120: "You don't make progress": "Remembering Shirley Chisholm: The First Black Woman to Run for President for the Democratic Party" [video], becauseofthemwecan.com, November 3, 2020.

Page 122: "For a moment": Douglas Martin, "She Ended the Men's Club of National Politics," *New York Times*, March 26, 2011.

Page 123: "as a possible successor": Lisa Lerer and Glenn Thrush, "Hillary Clinton's Bittersweet Return to the Democratic Convention," *New York Times*, August 19, 2020.

Page 125: "Your vote is your voice": Kamala Harris, Twitter, November 2, 2020.

Page 129: "I have no doubt": Savannah Walsh, "What Joe Biden and Kamala Harris Said during Their First Joint Appearance as Running Mates," *Elle*, August 12, 2020.

Page 132: "I accept your nomination": Matt Stevens, "Kamala Harris Accepts Vice-Presidential Nomination: Full Transcript," *New York Times*, August 19, 2020.

Page 140: "And protecting our democracy": "Read the transcript of Kamala Harris's victory speech in Wilmington, Del.," *Washington Post*, November 7, 2020.

Page 143: "Mr. Vice President": Susan Page, "Read the Full Transcript of Vice Presidential Debate between Mike Pence and Kamala Harris," *USA Today*, October 8, 2020.

Page 144: "And do you know": Page, "Read the Full Transcript."

Page 146: "Whether it's": Shikha Desai and Shamayita Chakraborty, "Dosas to Chicken Roast: Kamala Harris Cooks Her Way into America's Heart," *Times of India*, November 11, 2020.

Page 152: "The design symbolizes": Bria Goeller, "Statement on Ruby and Kamala," briagoeller.com.

Page 157: "My mother would look": Kamala Harris, "Homecoming Address," Spelman College, October 26, 2018.

Page 165: "When she takes": Elliott Davis, "Memorable Quotes from the Inauguration of Joe Biden and Kamala Harris," *US News*, January 20, 2021.

Page 169: "I, Kamala Devi Harris": Nadworny, "Kamala Harris Sworn In."

Page 170: "Emhoff chose to wear": Caroline Hallemann, "Second Gentleman Doug Emhoff Wore Ralph Lauren for the Inauguration," *Town and Country*, January 20, 2021.

Page 174: "Even in dark times": "Remarks by Vice President Kamala Harris at the Celebration of America," whitehouse.gov, January 20, 2021.

Page 182: "For many months": "COVID-19 Memorial Ceremony at Lincoln Memorial" [video], CSPAN, January 19, 2021.

PICTURE CREDITS

African American Museum and Library at Oakland, California, Photograph collection, MS 189, Oakland Public Library: 48.

Alamy: 84: Heidi Besen; **70:** © CBS/ZUMA Wire; **88:** Douglas Christian/ZUMA Wire/Alamy Live News; **6:** Loren Elliott; **106:** Brian Snyder/Reuters.

AP Images: 89: J. Scott Applewhite; **139:** Andrew Harnik; **78:** Fred Jewell; **67:** Carolyn Kaster; **ii:** John Locher; **60:** Ben Margot; **57:** George Nikitin; **74:** Rich Pedroncelli; **17:** Aijaz Rahi; **22:** RWK; **148:** Paul Sakuma; **65:** Marcio Jose Sanchez; **68:** Richard Shotwell/Invision.

Biden for President: 11.

DOD Photo: 100, 164, 167 by Navy Petty Officer 1st Class Carlos M. Vazquez II.

The English Montreal School Board and Westmount High School: 30, 31.

Photo attributed to **Jonathan Eubanks: 25.**

Courtesy **FCTRY.com: 151.**

Getty Images: 114, 129: Drew Angerer; **142:** Robyn Beck/AFP; **34:** Mary F. Calvert/MediaNews Group/*Mercury News*; **98:** Bill Clark/*CQ Roll Call*; **81:** Barbara Davidson/*Los Angeles Times*; **130:** Olivier Douliery/AFP; **108:** Al Drago; **154:** Demetrius Freeman/*Washington Post*; **90:** Zach Gibson; **168:** Andrew Harnik; **102:** Cliff Hawkins; **72:** Ralf-Finn Hestoft/Corbis; **44:** Marvin Joseph/*Washington Post*; **56 (top):** Mike Kepka/*San Francisco Chronicle*; **128:** Jeff Kowalsky/AFP; **87:** Saul Loeb via *Bloomberg*; **116:** Joshua Lott; **110:** Gabrielle Lurie/*San Francisco Chronicle*; **158:** Mark Makela; **112:** Melina Mara/*Washington Post*; **111:** Stephen Maturen; **140:** Win McNamee; **124:** Ethan Miller; **3:** Jeenah Moon/*Bloomberg*; **49:** Elijah Nouvelage/*Bloomberg*; **69:** Rich Polk/Getty Images for LACMA; **133:** Stephani Reynolds/*Bloomberg*; **175:** Joshua Roberts; **66:** Al Seib/*Los Angeles Times*; **182:** Chip Somodevilla; **105, 144:** Justin Sullivan; **123:** Allan Tannenbaum; **82, 92, 93:** Tom Williams/*CQ Roll Call*.

Courtesy of **Bria Goeller and Good Trubble (WTF America): 152.**

Patricia Montes Gregory via Flickr: **63.**

Inauguration Ladies © **Glen Hanson**, GlenHanson.com: **166.**

Courtesy **Allison Hoffman**, craftyiscool.com: **150.**

Courtesy of the **Joe Biden Campaign: 8.**

Kamala For Senate: 149.

Kamala Harris Campaign: 13, 15, 19, 20, 21, 27, 39.

Photo release courtesy of **Lauren Studios: 45.**

Library of Congress Prints and Photographs Division: 36: LC-USZ62-52494; **37:** The George F. Landegger Collection of District of Columbia Photographs in Carol M. Highsmith's America; **77:** Brady-Handy photograph collection/LCCN 2017895311; **121:** Thomas J. O'Halloran; **53:** ID 37245/Marion S. Trikosko.

Permission granted by SacSix, photo by **Christopher Measom: 153.**

Courtesy **National Archives**, ID no. 2803441/Yoichi R. Okamoto: **46.**

Office of Senator Kamala Harris: 73, 80, 96.

Courtesy of **Odette Pollar: 24.**

Redux Pictures: 156: Michelle V. Agins/*New York Times*; **118:** Joe Buglewicz/*New York Times*; **vi:** Tony Cenicola/*New York Times*; **79:** Nicole Craine/*New York Times*; **127:** Elizabeth Frantz/*New York Times*; **86:** T.J. Kirkpatrick/*New York Times*; **132:** Chris Lee/VII; **113:** Maddie McGarvey/*New York Times*; **147:** Melissa Melvin-Rodriguez/*New York Times*; **176:** Doug Mills/*New York Times*; **162:** Craig Ruttle; **32, 134, 159:** Erin Schaff/*New York Times*; **62:** Jim Wilson/*New York Times*; **94:** Damon Winter/*New York Times*.

Courtesy **Senate.gov: 178 (bottom).**

Shutterstock: 126: Michael F. Hiatt; **58:** Stephen Dorian Miner.

U.S. Army photo by Elizabeth Fraser: **172.**

Courtesy of **Yalda T. Uhls/Mina J. Bissell: 23.**

White House facebook page: **107.**

Official **White House** Photo: **170, 171:** Ana Isabel Martinez Chamorro; **174, 177, 178 (top), 180, 181:** Lawrence Jackson.